Texts in
Computing

Volume 7

Learn Prolog Now!

Volume 1
Programming Languages and Semantics
Maribel Fernandez

Volume 2
An Introduction to Lambda Calculus for Computer Scientists
Chris Hankin

Volume 3
Logical Reasoning: A First Course
Rob Nederpelt and Fairouz Kamareddine

Volume 4
The Haskell Road to Logic, Maths and Programming
Kees Doets and Jan van Eijck

Volume 5
Bridges from Classical to Nonmonotonic Reasoning
David Makinson

Volume 6
Automata and Dictionaries
Denis Maurel and Franz Guenthner

Volume 7
Learn Prolog Now!
Patrick Blackburn, Johan Bos and Kristina Striegnitz

Texts in Computing Series Editor
Ian Mackie   ian.mackie@kcl.ac.uk

Learn Prolog Now!

Patrick Blackburn
Johan Bos
Kristina Striegnitz

ISBN 1-904987-17-6
College Publications
Scientific Director: Dov Gabbay
Managing Director: Jane Spurr
Department of Computer Science
Strand, London WC2R 2LS, UK

Cover design by Richard Fraser, www.avalonarts.co.uk
Printed by Lightning Source, Milton Keynes, UK

Contents

Contents

Preface

Learn Prolog Now! has a long and twisted history. In 1995, all three
authors were based at the Department of Computational Linguistics, at
the University of the Saarland, in Saarbrücken, Germany. Johan, who
was teaching the introduction to Prolog that year, was working with
Patrick on a Prolog-based introduction to natural language semantics.[1]
He decided to prepare a short set of lecture notes on Prolog which
could also be used as an Appendix to the computational semantics book.

Nice idea, but that's not the way things worked out. First, between
1996 and 2000, Patrick and Johan rethought the structure of the Prolog
courses, and along the way the notes became book-sized. Then, from
2001 till 2004, Kristina took over the teaching, added new material and
(most importantly of all) turned *Learn Prolog Now!* into a web-book.

It quickly became apparent that we had a hit on our hands: the
website got up to 4,000 visitors a month, and we received many emails.
Actually, this put us in a bit of a quandary. We wanted to publish
Learn Prolog Now! as a (low-budget) book — but at the same time we
did *not* want a publisher telling us that we had to get rid of the free
online version.

Luckily, Vincent Hendricks came to the rescue (thanks Vincent!). He
told us about College Publications, Dov Gabbay's new publication house,
which was specifically designed to enable authors to retain copyright. It
was a marriage made in heaven. Thanks to College Publications we
could make *Learn Prolog Now!* available in book form at a reasonable
price, and keep the web-book in place.

And that's the book you're now reading. It has been thoroughly
tested, first on nearly a decade's worth of students at Saarbrücken, and at
the *16th European Summer School in Logic, Language and Information*
which took place in Nancy, France, in August 2004, where Kristina
taught a hands-on introduction to Prolog. Though, as we hope you will
swiftly discover, you *don't* need to be doing a course to follow this
book. We've tried to make *Learn Prolog Now!* self-contained and easy

---

[1]*Representation and Inference for Natural Language: A First Course in Computational
Semantics*, Patrick Blackburn and Johan Bos, CSLI Publications, 2005.

to follow, so that it can be used without a teacher. And as the feedback we have received confirms, this is one of the most popular ways of using it.

So — over to you. We had a lot of fun writing this. We hope you have a lot of fun reading it, and that it really will help you to learn Prolog now!

Acknowledgments

Over the years that *Learn Prolog Now!* existed as course notes and web-book, we received many emails, ranging from helpful comments to requests for answers to problems (a handful of which verged on demands that we do their homework assignments!). We can't thank everyone by name, but we did receive a lot of useful feedback this way and are very grateful. And if we did any homework assignments, we ain't telling...

We are extremely grateful to Gertjan van Noord and Robbert Prins, who used early versions of *Learn Prolog Now!* in their teaching at the University of Groningen. They gave us detailed feedback on its weak points, and we've tried to take their advice into account; we hope we've succeeded. We'd also like to say *Grazie!* to Malvina Nissim, who supplied us with an upgrade of Exercise 2.4, helped format the final hardcopy version, and generally gave us her enthusiastic support over many years.

Some special thanks are in order. First, we'd like to thank Dov Gabbay for founding College Publications; may it do for academic publishing what the GNU Public License did for software! Second, heartfelt thanks to Jane Spurr; we've *never* had a more helpful, competent, or enthusiastic editor, and *nobody* reacts faster than Jane. Thirdly, we like to thank Jan Wielemaker (the Linus Torvalds of the Prolog world) for making SWI Prolog freely available over the internet. SWI Prolog is a an ISO-compliant Free Software Prolog environment, licensed under the Lesser GNU Public License. We don't know what we'd have done without it. We're also very grateful to him for the speedy and informative feedback he gave us on a number of technical issues, and for encouraging us to go for ISO-standard Prolog. Finally, a big thank you to Ian Mackie and an anonymous referee for all the time and energy they put into the penultimate version of the book.

Patrick Blackburn
Johan Bos
Kristina Striegnitz
May 2006

Introduction

First off, what is Prolog? It's a programming language, but a rather unusual one. "Prolog" is short for "Programming with Logic", and though the link between logic and Prolog is not completely straightforward, it is this link that gives Prolog its special character. At the heart of Prolog lies a beautiful idea: don't tell the computer what to do, simply describe situations of interest. Where does the computation come in? When we ask questions. Prolog enables the computer to logically deduce new facts about the situations we describe, and gives its deductions back to us as answers.

This has a number of consequences. First, a practical one: if you are an experienced programmer, Prolog is likely to take you by surprise. It requires a different mindset. You have to learn to see computational problems from a different perspective. To use the standard terminology, you have to learn to think *declaratively*, rather than *procedurally*. This can be challenging, but it's also a lot of fun.

A second consequence of Prolog's "say what the problem *is*, rather than how to solve it" stance is that Prolog is a very high-level language. As will become apparent, Prolog enables you to describe some highly abstract things (for example, the syntactic structure of English) extremely succinctly. Moreover, these descriptions really are programs: they will do real work for us if we ask the right questions. For example, having described the syntactic structure of English, we can ask Prolog whether particular sentences are grammatical or not. Prolog will tell us, and if we ask the right question, will even give us a grammatical analysis.

Prolog's ability to describe complex situations succinctly means that it is good for rapid prototyping. That is, if you have a good idea, and want to get a working program that embodies it, Prolog is often an excellent choice. Ideas become computational reality fast with Prolog, at least for some applications. Which applications? Those which depend on getting to grips with rich structure. Prolog application areas include computational linguistics (or natural languages processing as it is often called), Artificial Intelligence (AI), expert systems, molecular biology, and the semantic web. Where there is structure to be described, or knowledge to be represented, Prolog is likely to come into its own.

Prolog is not a perfect language, and it's not suitable for everything. If you need to do serious text manipulation, go for Perl. If you need tight control over memory, go for C. If you want a mathematically elegant language that you can reason about easily, go for Caml, Haskell, or a clean Lisp dialect (such as Scheme). But no language is good for everything, and those that try (remember Ada?) often fall by the wayside. As we have just said, Prolog is a natural choice for knowledge-rich tasks, and there are a number of good reasons for learning it. If you are an experienced programmer, we think you will enjoy learning Prolog simply because it is so different; thinking declaratively, or almost declaratively, can send your brain in interesting new directions. And if you have little or no programing experience, and maybe aren't even sure if you like computers or not, then there are excellent reasons for choosing Prolog as your first language. Because it is so high-level, you get to do interesting things fast, without getting bogged down in tedious preparatory work. Moreover, you will swiftly learn about a number of fundamental programming concepts, notably recursion and recursive data structures, concepts that will be useful if you later study other languages. Finally, the link with logic adds an intriguing intellectual dimension to the learning process.

Where does Prolog come from? It originated in Marseilles, in the south of France. Alain Colmerauer and Philippe Roussel devised and implemented the first Prolog interpreter in 1972. One of the earliest versions was partially implemented in Fortran, and partially in Prolog itself. An interesting mixture: it would be hard to find two languages that differ more widely than the numerically oriented, non-recursive, imperative scientific programming language Fortran, and the symbolically oriented, recursive, declarative Prolog. A few years later, Robert Kowalski, who had worked with the Marseilles team in 1971 and 1972, published his book *Logic for Problem Solving*[1] which put the idea of logic programming firmly on the intellectual agenda. Another big step was taken in Edinburgh in 1977 with David Warren's implementation of the DEC 10 compiler.[2] This implementation, which could compete with (and sometimes surpass) state of the art Lisp implementations in terms of efficiency, turned Prolog from an academic curiosity into a serious programming language. Interesting work soon followed. For example,

---

[1]*Logic for Problem Solving*, R. Kowalski, Elsevier/North-Holland, 1979.
[2]David H. D. Warren, *Applied Logic — Its Use and Implementation as a Programming Tool*, PhD thesis, University of Edinburgh. Scotland, 1977.

in a classic paper, Pereira and Warren showed that Prolog's built-in mechanism for handling Definite Clause Grammars (DCGs) was a natural way of treating certain tasks in natural language processing.[3]

Since then, Prolog has grown in popularity, particularly in Europe and Japan (in the United States, work on AI has tended to be Lisp-based). Prolog is, was, and always will be, a niche language. But the niche it occupies is fascinating.

How to get the most out of this book

What we have said about Prolog so far has been high-level and abstract. We are now going to change gears. The approach taken to teaching Prolog in this book is *not* abstract, and is certainly *not* driven by high-level ideas (such as the link with logic). In fact, it's resolutely down to earth. We try to teach Prolog as concretely as possible. We've just told you why Prolog is not just another programming language, but we're going to teach it as if it was.

Why? Quite simply, because we think that's the best approach for a first course. Programming in Prolog is a practical skill. There are concrete things that simply have to be learned, and we strongly believe that you just have to get in there and learn them as fast as possible. This does not mean that we find the abstract side of Prolog (and more generally, logic programming) unimportant or uninteresting. However (unless you already have a good theoretical background) these deeper ideas take time to emerge clearly and be absorbed. In the meantime, you should be getting on with mastering the nuts and bolts.

To put it another way, we think that learning a programming language (any programming language, not just Prolog) is a lot like learning a foreign language. And what is the most important part of learning a foreign language? Actually *using* it, actually putting it to work, actually trying it out. Sure, reflecting on the beauty of the language is pleasant, but at the end of the day, what really counts is the time you spend on mastering the mechanics.

This attitude has strongly influenced the way *Learn Prolog Now!* is written. In particular, as you will see, each chapter is divided into three parts. First comes the text. Next come a number of exercises. Finally there is what we call the practical session. Now, we cannot emphasise the following point too strongly: *the practical sessions are the most important part of the book*. It is utterly imperative that you sit down,

---

[3]"Definite clause grammars for language analysis — a survey of the formalism and a comparison with augmented transition networks", F. Pereira and D. H. D. Warren, *Journal of Artificial Intelligence*, 13(3):231–278, 1980.

fire up a Prolog interpreter, and work through these sessions. Actually, just doing that is nowhere near enough. If you really want to master Prolog, you need to try out a lot more than is asked of you in these sessions. But we believe these sessions contain enough to put you on the right track.

Gaining practical experience with a programming language is always important, but, in our opinion, it is even more important than usual with Prolog. Why? Because Prolog is deceptively easy to understand. It's a small language (there are not a lot of constructs to learn) and the basic ideas are beautiful in their simplicity. It is dangerously easy to smile, relax, and say "'Hey! I get it!'". Easy, but wrong. The basic ideas interact in subtle ways, and without *lots* of practical experience you will be lost. We have had many (very bright) students who thought they understood it, didn't put in the effort on the practical side — and who later found themselves scrambling to keep up. Prolog is subtle. You need to put in the hours if you want to master it.

Summing up, *Learn Prolog Now* is a practically oriented introduction to the central features of Prolog. It won't teach you everything, but if you make it to the end you'll have a good grasp of the basics, and will have caught a glimpse of what logic programming is about. Enjoy!

Chapter 1

Facts, Rules, and Queries

This chapter has two main goals:

1. To give some simple examples of Prolog programs. This will introduce us to the three basic constructs in Prolog: facts, rules, and queries. It will also introduce us to a number of other themes, like the role of logic in Prolog, and the idea of performing unification with the aid of variables.

2. To begin the systematic study of Prolog by defining terms, atoms, variables and other syntactic concepts.

1 Some Simple Examples

There are only three basic constructs in Prolog: facts, rules, and queries. A collection of facts and rules is called a knowledge base (or a database) and Prolog programming is all about writing knowledge bases. That is, Prolog programs simply *are* knowledge bases, collections of facts and rules which describe some collection of relationships that we find interesting.

So how do we *use* a Prolog program? By posing queries. That is, by asking questions about the information stored in the knowledge base.

Now this probably sounds rather strange. It's certainly not obvious that it has much to do with programming at all. After all, isn't programming all about telling a computer what to do? But as we shall see, the Prolog way of programming makes a lot of sense, at least for certain tasks; for example, it is useful in computational linguistics and Artificial Intelligence (AI). But instead of saying more about Prolog in general terms, let's jump right in and start writing some simple knowledge bases; this is not just the best way of learning Prolog, it's the only way.

Knowledge Base 1

Knowledge Base 1 (KB1) is simply a collection of facts. Facts are used to state things that are *unconditionally* true of some situation of interest. For example, we can state that Mia, Jody, and Yolanda are women, that Jody plays air guitar, and that a party is taking place, using the following five facts:

```
woman(mia).
woman(jody).
woman(yolanda).
playsAirGuitar(jody).
party.
```

This collection of facts is KB1. It is our first example of a Prolog program. Note that the names mia, jody, and yolanda, the properties woman and playsAirGuitar, and the proposition party have been written so that the first letter is in lower-case. This is important; we will see why a little later on.

How can we use KB1? By posing queries. That is, by asking questions about the information KB1 contains. Here are some examples. We can ask Prolog whether Mia is a woman by posing the query:

```
?- woman(mia).
```

Prolog will answer

(margin notes: knowledge base, database, facts, queries)

```
yes
```

for the obvious reason that this is one of the facts explicitly recorded in KB1. Incidentally, *we* don't type in the ?-. This symbol (or something like it, depending on the implementation of Prolog you are using) is the prompt symbol that the Prolog interpreter displays when it is waiting to evaluate a query. We just type in the actual query (for example woman(mia)) followed by . (a full stop). The full stop is important. If you don't type it, Prolog won't start working on the query.

Similarly, we can ask whether Jody plays air guitar by posing the following query:

```
?- playsAirGuitar(jody).
```

Prolog will again answer yes, because this is one of the facts in KB1. However, suppose we ask whether Mia plays air guitar:

```
?- playsAirGuitar(mia).
```

We will get the answer

```
no
```

Why? Well, first of all, this is not a fact in KB1. Moreover, KB1 is extremely simple, and contains no other information (such as the *rules* we will learn about shortly) which might help Prolog try to infer (that is, deduce) whether Mia plays air guitar. So Prolog correctly concludes that playsAirGuitar(mia) does *not* follow from KB1.

| infer |
| deduce |

Here are two important examples. First, suppose we pose the query:

```
?- playsAirGuitar(vincent).
```

Again Prolog answers no. Why? Well, this query is about a person (Vincent) that it has no information about, so it (correctly) concludes that playsAirGuitar(vincent) cannot be deduced from the information in KB1.

Similarly, suppose we pose the query:

```
?- tatooed(jody).
```

Again Prolog will answer no. Why? Well, this query is about a property (being tatooed) that it has no information about, so once again it (correctly) concludes that the query cannot be deduced from the information in KB1. (Actually, some Prolog implementations will respond to this query with an error message, telling you that the predicate or procedure tatooed is not defined; we will soon introduce the notion of predicates.)

Needless to say, we can also make queries concerning propositions. For example, if we pose the query

```
?- party.
```

then Prolog will respond

```
yes
```

and if we pose the query

```
?- rockConcert.
```

then Prolog will respond

```
no
```

exactly as we would expect.

Knowledge Base 2

Here is KB2, our second knowledge base:

```
happy(yolanda).
listens2Music(mia).
listens2Music(yolanda):- happy(yolanda).
playsAirGuitar(mia):- listens2Music(mia).
playsAirGuitar(yolanda):- listens2Music(yolanda).
```

> rules

There are two facts in KB2, listens2Music(mia) and happy(yolanda). The last three items it contains are rules.

Rules state information that is *conditionally* true of the situation of interest. For example, the first rule says that Yolanda listens to music *if* she is happy, and the last rule says that Yolanda plays air guitar *if* she listens to music. More generally, the :- should be read as "if", or "is implied by". The part on the left hand side of the :- is called the

> head

head of the rule, the part on the right hand side is called the body. So

> body

in general rules say: *if* the body of the rule is true, *then* the head of the rule is true too. And now for the key point:

> *If a knowledge base contains a rule* head :- body, *and Prolog knows that* body *follows from the information in the knowledge base, then Prolog can infer* head.

> modus
> ponens

This fundamental deduction step is called modus ponens.

Let's consider an example. Suppose we ask whether Mia plays air guitar:

```
?- playsAirGuitar(mia).
```

Prolog will respond yes. Why? Well, although it can't find
playsAirGuitar(mia) as a fact explicitly recorded in KB2, it can find
the rule

```
playsAirGuitar(mia):- listens2Music(mia).
```

Moreover, KB2 also contains the fact listens2Music(mia). Hence Prolog
can use the rule of modus ponens to deduce that playsAirGuitar(mia).
   Our next example shows that Prolog can chain together uses of modus
ponens. Suppose we ask:

```
?- playsAirGuitar(yolanda).
```

Prolog would respond yes. Why? Well, first of all, by using the fact
happy(yolanda) and the rule

```
listens2Music(yolanda):- happy(yolanda).
```

Prolog can deduce the new fact listens2Music(yolanda). This new
fact is not explicitly recorded in the knowledge base — it is only
implicitly present (it is *inferred* knowledge). Nonetheless, Prolog can
then use it just like an explicitly recorded fact. In particular, from this
inferred fact and the rule

```
playsAirGuitar(yolanda):- listens2Music(yolanda).
```

it can deduce playsAirGuitar(yolanda), which is what we asked it.
Summing up: any fact produced by an application of modus ponens can
be used as input to further rules. By chaining together applications of
modus ponens in this way, Prolog is able to retrieve information that
logically follows from the rules and facts recorded in the knowledge
base.
   The facts and rules contained in a knowledge base are called clauses.   clauses
Thus KB2 contains five clauses, namely three rules and two facts.
Another way of looking at KB2 is to say that it consists of three
predicates (or procedures). The three predicates are: predicates

                                                                           procedures

```
listens2Music
happy
playsAirGuitar
```

The happy predicate is defined using a single clause (a fact). The
listens2Music and playsAirGuitar predicates are each defined using

two clauses (in one case, two rules, and in the other case, one rule and one fact). It is a good idea to think about Prolog programs in terms of the predicates they contain. In essence, the predicates are the concepts we find important, and the various clauses we write down concerning them are our attempts to pin down what they mean and how they are inter-related.

One final remark. We can view a fact as a rule with an empty body. That is, we can think of facts as conditionals that do not have any antecedent conditions, or degenerate rules.

Knowledge Base 3

KB3, our third knowledge base, consists of five clauses:

```
happy(vincent).
listens2Music(butch).
playsAirGuitar(vincent):-
    listens2Music(vincent),
    happy(vincent).
playsAirGuitar(butch):-
    happy(butch).
playsAirGuitar(butch):-
    listens2Music(butch).
```

There are two facts, happy(vincent) and listens2Music(butch), and three rules.

KB3 defines the same three predicates as KB2 (namely happy, listens2Music, and playsAirGuitar) but it defines them differently. In particular, the three rules that define the playsAirGuitar predicate introduce some new ideas. First, note that the rule

```
playsAirGuitar(vincent):-
    listens2Music(vincent),
    happy(vincent).
```

goals

has *two* items in its body, or (to use the standard terminology) two goals. So, what exactly does this rule mean? The most important thing to note is the comma , that separates the goal listens2Music(vincent) and the goal happy(vincent) in the rule's body. This is the way logical conjunction is expressed in Prolog (that is, the comma means *and*). So this rule says: "Vincent plays air guitar if he listens to music *and* he is happy".

conjunction

Thus, if we posed the query

```
?- playsAirGuitar(vincent).
```

Prolog would answer no. This is because while KB3 contains happy(vincent), it does *not* explicitly contain the information listens2Music(vincent), and this fact cannot be deduced either. So KB3 only fulfils one of the two preconditions needed to establish playsAirGuitar(vincent), and our query fails.

Incidentally, the spacing used in this rule is irrelevant. For example, we could have written it as

```
playsAirGuitar(vincent):- happy(vincent),
                          listens2Music(vincent).
```

and it would have meant exactly the same thing. Prolog offers us a lot of freedom in the way we set out knowledge bases, and we can take advantage of this to keep our code readable.

Next, note that KB3 contains two rules with *exactly* the same head, namely:

```
playsAirGuitar(butch):-
    happy(butch).
playsAirGuitar(butch):-
    listens2Music(butch).
```

This is a way of stating that Butch plays air guitar *either* if he listens to music, *or* if he is happy. That is, listing multiple rules with the same head is a way of expressing logical disjunction (that is, it is a way of saying *or*). So if we posed the query

| disjunction |

```
?- playsAirGuitar(butch).
```

Prolog would answer yes. For although the first of these rules will not help (KB3 does not allow Prolog to conclude that happy(butch)), KB3 *does* contain listens2Music(butch) and this means Prolog can apply modus ponens using the rule

```
playsAirGuitar(butch):-
    listens2Music(butch).
```

to conclude that playsAirGuitar(butch).

There is another way of expressing disjunction in Prolog. We could replace the pair of rules given above by the single rule

```
playsAirGuitar(butch):-
    happy(butch);
    listens2Music(butch).
```

That is, the semicolon ; is the Prolog symbol for *or*, so this single rule means exactly the same thing as the previous pair of rules. Is it better to use multiple rules or the semicolon? That depends. On the one hand, extensive use of semicolon can make Prolog code hard to read. On the other hand, the semicolon is more efficient as Prolog only has to deal with one rule.

logic

It should now be clear that Prolog has something to do with logic: after all, the :- means implication, the , means conjunction, and the ; means disjunction. (What about negation? That is a whole other story. We'll be discussing it in Chapter 10.) Moreover, we have seen that a standard logical proof rule (modus ponens) plays an important role in Prolog programming. So we are already beginning to understand why "Prolog" is short for "Programming with logic".

Knowledge Base 4

Here is KB4, our fourth knowledge base:

```
woman(mia).
woman(jody).
woman(yolanda).

loves(vincent,mia).
loves(marsellus,mia).
loves(pumpkin,honey_bunny).
loves(honey_bunny,pumpkin).
```

Now, this is a pretty boring knowledge base. There are no rules, only a collection of facts. Ok, we are seeing a relation that has two names as arguments for the first time (namely the loves relation), but, let's face it, that's a rather predictable idea.

No, the novelty this time lies not in the knowledge base, it lies in the queries we are going to pose. In particular, *for the first time we're*

variables

going to make use of variables. Here's an example:

```
?- woman(X).
```

The X is a variable (in fact, any word beginning with an upper-case letter is a Prolog variable, which is why we had to be careful to use lower-case initial letters in our earlier examples). Now a variable isn't a name, rather it's a *placeholder* for information. That is, this query asks Prolog: tell me which of the individuals you know about is a woman.

Prolog answers this query by working its way through KB4, from top to bottom, trying to unify (or match) the expression woman(X) with the information KB4 contains. Now the first item in the knowledge base is woman(mia). So, Prolog unifies X with mia, thus making the query agree perfectly with this first item. (Incidentally, there's a lot of different terminology for this process: we can also say that Prolog instantiates X to mia, or that it binds X to mia.) Prolog then reports back to us as follows:

unify

match

instantiates

binds

    X = mia

That is, it not only says that there is information about at least one woman in KB4, it actually tells us who she is. It didn't just say yes, it actually gave us the variable binding (or variable instantiation) that led to success.

But that's not the end of the story. The whole point of variables is that they can stand for, or unify with, different things. And there is information about other women in the knowledge base. We can access this information by typing a semicolon:

variable binding

variable instantiation

    X = mia ;

Remember that ; means *or*, so this query means: *are there any alternatives*? So Prolog begins working through the knowledge base again (it remembers where it got up to last time and starts from there) and sees that if it unifies X with jody, then the query agrees perfectly with the second entry in the knowledge base. So it responds:

    X = mia ;
    X = jody

It's telling us that there is information about a second woman in KB4, and (once again) it actually gives us the value that led to success. And of course, if we press ; a second time, Prolog returns the answer

    X = mia ;
    X = jody ;
    X = yolanda

But what happens if we press ; a *third* time? Prolog responds no. No other unifications are possible. There are no other facts starting with the symbol woman. The last four entries in the knowledge base concern the love relation, and there is no way that such entries can be unified with a query of the form of the form woman(X).

Let's try a more complicated query, namely

```
?- loves(marsellus,X), woman(X).
```

Now, remember that , means *and*, so this query says: *is there any individual* X *such that Marcellus loves* X *and* X *is a woman*? If you look at the knowledge base you'll see that there is: Mia is a woman (fact 1) and Marcellus loves Mia (fact 5). And in fact, Prolog is capable of working this out. That is, it can search through the knowledge base and work out that if it unifies X with Mia, then both conjuncts of the query are satisfied (we'll learn in the following chapter how Prolog does this). So Prolog returns the answer

```
X = mia
```

The business of unifying variables with information in the knowledge base is the heart of Prolog. As we'll learn, there are many interesting ideas in Prolog — but when you get right down to it, it's Prolog's ability to perform unification and return the values of the variable bindings to us that is crucial.

Knowledge Base 5

Well, we've introduced variables, but so far we've only used them in queries. But variables not only *can* be used in knowledge bases, it's only when we start to do so that we can write truly interesting programs. Here's a simple example, the knowledge base KB5:

```
loves(vincent,mia).
loves(marsellus,mia).
loves(pumpkin,honey_bunny).
loves(honey_bunny,pumpkin).

jealous(X,Y):- loves(X,Z), loves(Y,Z).
```

KB5 contains four facts about the loves relation and one rule. (Incidentally, the blank line between the facts and the rule has no meaning: it's simply there to increase the readability. As we said earlier, Prolog gives us a great deal of freedom in the way we format knowledge bases.) But this rule is by far the most interesting one we have seen so far: it contains three variables (note that X, Y, and Z are all upper-case letters). What does it say?

In effect, it is defining a concept of jealousy. It says that an individual X will be jealous of an individual Y if there is some individual Z that X loves, and Y loves that same individual Z too. (Ok, so jealously isn't as straightforward as this in the real world.) The key thing to note is that this is a *general* statement: it is not stated in terms of mia, or pumpkin, or anyone in particular — it's a conditional statement about *everybody* in our little world.

Suppose we pose the query:

```
?- jealous(marsellus,W).
```

This query asks: can you find an individual W such that Marcellus is jealous of W? Vincent is such an individual. If you check the definition of jealousy, you'll see that Marcellus must be jealous of Vincent, because they both love the same woman, namely Mia. So Prolog will return the value

```
W = vincent
```

Now some questions for *you*. First, are there any other jealous people in KB5? Furthermore, suppose we wanted Prolog to tell us about all the jealous people: what query would we pose? Do any of the answers surprise you? Do any seem silly?

2 Prolog Syntax

Now that we've got some idea of what Prolog does, it's time to go back to the beginning and work through the details more carefully. Let's start by asking a very basic question: we've seen all kinds of expressions (for example jody, playsAirGuitar(mia), and X) in our Prolog programs, but these have just been examples. It's time for precision: exactly what are facts, rules, and queries built out of?

The answer is terms, and there are four kinds of term in Prolog: atoms, numbers, variables, and complex terms (or structures). Atoms and numbers are lumped together under the heading constants, and constants and variables together make up the simple terms of Prolog.

Let's take a closer look. To make things crystal clear, let's first be precise about the basic characters (that is, symbols) at our disposal. The *upper-case letters* are A, B,...,Z; the *lower-case letters* are a, b,...,z; the *digits* are 1, 2,...,9. In addition we have the _ symbol, which is called underscore, and some *special characters*, which include characters such as +, -, *, /, <, >, =, :, ., &, ~. The blank *space* is also a character, but a rather unusual one, being invisible. A string is an unbroken sequence of characters.

Atoms

An atom is either:

terms

constants

simple terms

characters

underscore

string

atom

1. A string of characters made up of upper-case letters, lower-case letters, digits, and the underscore character, that begins with a lower-case letter. Here are some examples: `butch`, `big_kahuna_burger`, `listens2Music` and `playsAirGuitar`.

2. An arbitrary sequence of characters enclosed in single quotes. For example `'Vincent'`, `'The Gimp'`, `'Five_Dollar_Shake'`, `'&^%&#@$ &*'`, and `' '`. The sequence of characters between the single quotes is called the atom name. Note that we are allowed to use spaces in such atoms; in fact, a common reason for using single quotes is so we can do precisely that.

| atom name |

3. A string of special characters. Here are some examples: `@=` and `====>` and `;` and `:-` are all atoms. As we have seen, some of these atoms, such as `;` and `:-` have a pre-defined meaning.

Numbers

| numbers |

| floating point |

| floats |

| integers |

Real numbers aren't particularly important in typical Prolog applications. So although most Prolog implementations do support floating point numbers or floats (that is, representations of real numbers such as 1657.3087 or π) we say little about them in this book.

But integers (that is: ...,-2, -1, 0, 1, 2, 3,...) are useful for such tasks as counting the elements of a list, and we'll discuss how to manipulate them in Chapter 5. Their Prolog syntax is the obvious one: 23, 1001, 0, -365, and so on.

Variables

| variable |

A variable is a string of upper-case letters, lower-case letters, digits and underscore characters that starts *either* with an upper-case letter *or* with an underscore. For example, X, Y, Variable, _tag, X_526, List, List24, _head, Tail, _input and Output are all Prolog variables.

The variable _ (that is, a single underscore character) is rather special. It's called the *anonymous variable*, and we discuss it in Chapter 4.

Complex terms

| complex terms |

| structures |

| functor |

| arguments |

Constants, numbers, and variables are the building blocks: now we need to know how to fit them together to make complex terms. Recall that complex terms are often called structures.

Complex terms are build out of a functor followed by a sequence of arguments. The arguments are put in ordinary parentheses, separated by commas, and placed after the functor. Note that the functor has to be directly followed by the parenthesis; you can't have a space between the functor and the parenthesis enclosing the arguments. The functor *must* be an atom. That is, variables *cannot* be used as functors. On the other hand, arguments can be any kind of term.

Now, we've already seen lots of examples of complex terms when we looked at the knowledge bases KB1 to KB5. For example, `playsAirGuitar(jody)` is a complex term: its functor is `playsAirGuitar` and its argument is `jody`. Other examples are `loves(vincent,mia)` and, to give an example containing a variable, `jealous(marsellus,W)`.

But the definition allows for more complex terms than this. In fact, it allows us to keep nesting complex terms inside complex terms indefinitely (that is, it is allows recursive structure). For example

> recursive structure

```
hide(X,father(father(father(butch))))
```

is a perfectly acceptable complex term. Its functor is `hide`, and it has two arguments: the variable `X`, and the complex term `father(father(father(butch)))`. This complex term has `father` as its functor, and another complex term, namely `father(father(butch))`, as its sole argument. And the argument of this complex term, namely `father(butch)`, is also complex. But then the nesting bottoms out, for the argument here is the constant `butch`.

As we shall see, such nested (or recursively structured) terms enable us to represent many problems naturally. In fact the interplay between recursive term structure and variable unification is the source of much of Prolog's power.

The number of arguments that a complex term has is called its arity. For example, `woman(mia)` is a complex term of arity 1, and `loves(vincent,mia)` is a complex term of arity 2.

> arity

Arity is important to Prolog. Prolog would be quite happy for us to define two predicates with the same functor but with a different number of arguments. For example, we are free to define a knowledge base that defines a two-place predicate `love` (this might contain such facts as `love(vincent,mia)`), and also a three-place `love` predicate (which might contain such facts as `love(vincent,marsellus,mia)`). However, if we did this, Prolog would treat the two-place `love` and the three-place `love` as different predicates. Later in the book (for example, when we introduce accumulators in Chapter 5) we shall see that it can be useful to define two predicates with the same functor but different arity.

When we need to talk about predicates and how we intend to use them (for example, in documentation) it is usual to use a suffix / followed by a number to indicate the predicate's arity. To return to KB2, instead of saying that it defines predicates

```
listens2Music
happy
playsAirGuitar
```

we should really say that it defines predicates

```
listens2Music/1
happy/1
playsAirGuitar/1
```

And Prolog can't get confused about a knowledge base containing the two different love predicates, for it regards the `love/2` predicate and the `love/3` predicate as distinct.

3 Exercises

Exercise 1.1.   Which of the following sequences of characters are atoms, which are variables, and which are neither?

1. `vINCENT`

2. `Footmassage`

3. `variable23`

4. `Variable2000`

5. `big_kahuna_burger`

6. `'big kahuna burger'`

7. `big kahuna burger`

8. `'Jules'`

9. `_Jules`

10. `'_Jules'`

Exercise 1.2.   Which of the following sequences of characters are atoms, which are variables, which are complex terms, and which are not terms at all? Give the functor and arity of each complex term.

1. `loves(Vincent,mia)`

2. `'loves(Vincent,mia)'`

3. Butch(boxer)

4. boxer(Butch)

5. and(big(burger),kahuna(burger))

6. and(big(X),kahuna(X))

7. _and(big(X),kahuna(X))

8. (Butch kills Vincent)

9. kills(Butch Vincent)

10. kills(Butch,Vincent

Exercise 1.3. How many facts, rules, clauses, and predicates are there in the following knowledge base? What are the heads of the rules, and what are the goals they contain?

```
woman(vincent).
woman(mia).
man(jules).
person(X):- man(X); woman(X).
loves(X,Y):- father(X,Y).
father(Y,Z):- man(Y), son(Z,Y).
father(Y,Z):- man(Y), daughter(Z,Y).
```

Exercise 1.4. Represent the following in Prolog:

1. Butch is a killer.

2. Mia and Marcellus are married.

3. Zed is dead.

4. Marcellus kills everyone who gives Mia a footmassage.

5. Mia loves everyone who is a good dancer.

6. Jules eats anything that is nutritious or tasty.

Exercise 1.5. Suppose we are working with the following knowledge base:

```
wizard(ron).
hasWand(harry).
quidditchPlayer(harry).
wizard(X):- hasBroom(X), hasWand(X).
hasBroom(X):- quidditchPlayer(X).
```

How does Prolog respond to the following queries?

1. `wizard(ron).`

2. `witch(ron).`

3. `wizard(hermione).`

4. `witch(hermione).`

5. `wizard(harry).`

6. `wizard(Y).`

7. `witch(Y).`

4 Practical Session

Don't be fooled by the fact that the description of the practical sessions
is shorter than the text you have just read; the practical part is definitely
the most important. Yes, you need to read the text and do the exercises,
but that's not enough to become a Prolog programmer. To really master
the language you need to sit down in front of a computer and play with
Prolog — a lot!

The goal of the first practical session is for you to become familiar
with the basics of how to create and run simple Prolog programs. Now,
because there are many different implementations of Prolog, and different
operating systems you can run them under, we can't be too specific
here. Rather, what we'll do is describe in very general terms what is
involved in running Prolog, list the practical skills you need to master,
and suggest some things for you to do.

The simplest way to run a Prolog program is as follows. You have
a file with your Prolog program in it (for example, you may have a
file kb2.pl which contains the knowledge base KB2). You then start
Prolog. Prolog will display its prompt, something like

```
?-
```

which indicates that it is ready to accept a query.

Now, at this stage, Prolog knows absolutely nothing about KB2 (or indeed anything else). To see this, type in the command listing, followed by a full stop, and hit return. That is, type

    ?- listing.

and press the return key.

Now, the listing command is a special built-in Prolog predicate that | listing |
instructs Prolog to display the contents of the current knowledge base. But we haven't yet told Prolog about any knowledge bases, so it will just say

    yes

This is a correct answer: as yet Prolog knows nothing — so it correctly displays all this nothing and says yes. Actually, with more sophisticated Prolog implementations you may get a little more (for example, the names of libraries that have been loaded; libraries are discussed in Chapter 12) but, one way or another, you will receive what is essentially an "I know nothing about any knowledge bases!" answer.

So let's tell Prolog about KB2. Assuming that you've stored KB2 in the file kb2.pl, and that this file is in the directory where you're running Prolog, all you have to type is

    ?- [kb2].

This tells Prolog to consult the file kb2.pl, and load the contents as its | consult |
new knowledge base. Assuming that kb2.pl contains no typos, Prolog will read it in, maybe print out a message saying that it is consulting this file, and then answer:

    yes

Incidentally, it is common to store Prolog code in files with a .pl suffix. It's an indication of what the file contains (namely Prolog code) and with some Prolog implementations you don't actually have to type in the .pl suffix when you consult a file. Nice — but there is a drawback. Files containing Perl scripts usually have a .pl suffix too, and nowadays there are a lot of Perl scripts in use, so this can cause confusion. C'est la vie.

If the above doesn't work, that is, if typing

    ?- [kb2].

produces an error message saying that the file `kb2` does not exist, then you probably haven't started Prolog from the directory where `kb2.pl` is stored. In that case, you can either stop Prolog (by typing `halt.` after the prompt), change to the directory where `kb2.pl` is stored, and start Prolog again. Or you can tell Prolog exactly where to look for `kb2.pl`. To do this, instead of writing only `kb2` between the square brackets, you give Prolog the whole path enclosed in single quotes. For example, you type something like

```
?- ['home/kris/Prolog/kb2.pl'].
```

or

```
?- ['c:/Documents and Settings/Kris/Prolog/kb2.pl'].
```

Ok, so Prolog should now know about all the KB2 predicates. And we can check whether it does by using the `listing` command again:

```
?- listing.
```

If you do this, Prolog will list (something like) the following on the screen:

```
listens2Music(mia).
happy(yolanda).
playsAirGuitar(mia):-
    listens2Music(mia).
playsAirGuitar(yolanda):-
    listens2Music(yolanda).
listens2Music(yolanda):-
    happy(yolanda).

yes
```

That is, it will list the facts and rules that make up KB2, and then say yes. Once again, you may get a little more than this, such as the locations of various libraries that have been loaded.

Incidentally, `listing` can be used in other ways. For example, typing

```
?- listing(playsAirGuitar).
```

simply lists all the information in the knowledge base about the `playsAirGuitar` predicate. So in this case Prolog will display

```
playsAirGuitar(mia):-
    listens2Music(mia).
playsAirGuitar(yolanda):-
    listens2Music(yolanda).
```

```
yes
```

Well — now you're ready to go. KB2 is loaded and Prolog is running, so you can (and should!) start making exactly the sort of inquiries we discussed in the text.

But let's back up a little, and summarise a few of the practical skills you will need to master to get this far:

- You will need to know some basic facts about the operating system you are using, such as the directory structure it uses. After all, you will need to know how to save the files containing programs where you want them.

- You will need to know how to use some sort of text editor, in order to write and modify programs. Some Prolog implementations come with built-in text editors, but if you already know a text editor (such as Emacs) you can use this to write your Prolog code. Just make sure that you save your files as simple text files (for example, if you are working under Windows, don't save them as Word documents).

- You may want to take example Prolog programs from the internet. So make sure you know how to use a browser to find what you want, and to store the code where you want it.

- You need to know how to start your version of Prolog, and how to consult files with it.

The sooner you pick up these skills, the better. With them out of the way (which shouldn't take long) you can start concentrating on mastering Prolog (which will take longer).

But assuming you have mastered these skills, what next? Quite simply, *play with Prolog!* Consult the various knowledge bases discussed in the text, and check that the queries discussed really do work the way we said they did. In particular, take a look at KB5 and make sure you understand why you get those peculiar jealousy relations. Try posing new queries. Experiment with the `listing` predicate (it's a useful tool). Type in the knowledge base used in Exercise 1.5, and check whether your answers are correct. Best of all, think of some simple situation that interests you, and create a brand-new knowledge base from scratch.

Chapter 2

Unification and Proof Search

This chapter has two main goals:

1. To discuss unification in Prolog, and to explain how Prolog unification differs from standard unification. Along the way, we'll introduce =/2, the built-in predicate for Prolog unification, and unify_with_occurs_check/2, the built-in predicate for standard unification.

2. To explain the search strategy Prolog uses when it tries to deduce new information from old using modus ponens.

1   Unification

When working with knowledge base KB4 in the previous chapter, we
briefly mentioned the idea of unification. We said, for example, that
Prolog unifies woman(X) with woman(mia), thereby instantiating the
variable X to mia. It's now time to take a closer look at unification, for
it is one of the most fundamental ideas in Prolog.

unification

instantiating

Recall that there are three types of term:

1. Constants. These can either be atoms (such as vincent) or
   numbers (such as 24).

2. Variables. (Such as X, Z3, and List.)

3. Complex terms. These have the form:
   functor(term_1,...,term_n).

We are going to work our way towards a definition of when Prolog
will unify two terms. Our starting point will be the following working
definition. It gives the basic intuition, but is a little light on detail:

*Two terms unify if they are the same term or if they contain
variables that can be uniformly instantiated with terms in such a
way that the resulting terms are equal.*

This means, for example, that the terms mia and mia unify, because
they are the same atom. Similarly, the terms 42 and 42 unify, because
they are the same number, the terms X and X unify, because they are
the same variable, and the terms woman(mia) and woman(mia) unify,
because they are the same complex term. The terms woman(mia) and
woman(vincent), however, do not unify, as they are not the same (and
neither of them contains a variable that could be instantiated to make
them the same).

Now, what about the terms mia and X? They are not the same.
However, the variable X can be instantiated to mia which makes them
equal. So, by the second part of our working definition, mia and X unify.
Similarly, the terms woman(X) and woman(mia) unify, because they can
be made equal by instantiating X to mia. How about loves(vincent,X)
and loves(X,mia)? No. It is impossible to find an instantiation of
X that makes the two terms equal. Do you see why? Instantiating
X to vincent would give us the terms loves(vincent,vincent)
and loves(vincent,mia), which are obviously not equal. However,
instantiating X to mia, would yield the terms loves(vincent,mia) and
loves(mia,mia), which aren't equal either.

Usually we are not only interested in the fact that two terms unify, we also want to know how the variables have to be instantiated to make them equal. And Prolog gives us this information. When Prolog unifies two terms it performs all the necessary instantiations, so that the terms really are equal afterwards. This functionality, together with the fact that we are allowed to build complex terms (that is, recursively structured terms) makes unification a powerful programming mechanism.

instantia-
tions

recursively
structured

The basic intuitions should now be clear. Here's the definition which makes them precise. It tells us not only which terms Prolog will unify, but also what it will do to the variables to achieve this.

1. *If* `term1` *and* `term2` *are constants, then* `term1` *and* `term2` *unify if and only if they are the same atom, or the same number.*

2. *If* `term1` *is a variable and* `term2` *is any type of term, then* `term1` *and* `term2` *unify, and* `term1` *is instantiated to* `term2`. *Similarly, if* `term2` *is a variable and* `term1` *is any type of term, then* `term1` *and* `term2` *unify, and* `term2` *is instantiated to* `term1`. *(So if they are both variables, they're both instantiated to each other, and we say that they share values.)*

share
values

3. *If* `term1` *and* `term2` *are complex terms, then they unify if and only if:*

   (a) *They have the same functor and arity, and*

   (b) *all their corresponding arguments unify, and*

   (c) *the variable instantiations are compatible. (For example, it is not possible to instantiate variable* X *to* `mia` *when unifying one pair of arguments, and to instantiate* X *to* `vincent` *when unifying another pair of arguments.)*

4. *Two terms unify if and only if it follows from the previous three clauses that they unify.*

Let's have a look at the form of this definition. The first clause tells us when two constants unify. The second clause tells us when two terms, one of which is a variable, unify (such terms will always unify; variables unify with *anything*). Just as importantly, this clause also tells what instantiations we have to perform to make the two terms the same. Finally, the third clause tells us when two complex terms unify. Note the structure of this definition. Its first three clauses mirror perfectly the (recursive) structure of terms.

The fourth clause is also important: it says that the first three clauses tell us all we need to know about the unification of two terms. If two terms can't be shown to unify using clauses 1–3, then they *don't* unify. For example, batman does not unify with daughter(ink). Why not? Well, the first term is a constant, and the second is a complex term. But none of the first three clauses tell us how to unify two such terms, hence (by clause 4) they don't unify.

Examples

To make sure we've fully understood this definition, let's work through several examples. In these examples we'll make use of an important built-in predicate, the =/2 predicate (recall that writing /2 at the end indicates that this predicate takes two arguments).

The =/2 predicate tests whether its two arguments unify. For example, if we pose the query

```
?- =(mia,mia).
```

Prolog will respond yes, and if we pose the query

```
?- =(mia,vincent).
```

Prolog will respond no.

But we usually wouldn't pose these queries in quite this way. Let's face it, the notation =(mia,mia) is rather unnatural. It would be nicer if we could use infix notation (that is, if we could put the =/2 functor between its arguments) and write things like:

```
?- mia = mia.
```

In fact, Prolog lets us do this, so in the examples that follow we'll use infix notation.

Let's return to our first example:

```
?- mia = mia.
yes
```

Why does Prolog say yes? This may seem like a silly question: surely it's obvious that the terms unify! That's true, but how does this follow from the definition given above? It is important to learn to think systematically about unification (it is utterly fundamental to Prolog), and thinking systematically means relating the examples to the definition of unification given above. So let's think this example through.

The definition has three clauses. Now, clause 2 is for when one argument is a variable, and clause 3 is for when both arguments are complex terms, so these are of no use here. However clause 1 *is* relevant to our example. This tells us that two constants unify if and only if they are exactly the same object. As mia and mia are the same atom, unification succeeds.

A similar argument explains the following responses:

```
?- 2 = 2.
yes

?- mia = vincent.
no
```

Once again, clause 1 is relevant here (after all, 2, mia, and vincent are all constants). And as 2 is the same number as 2, and as mia is *not* the same atom as vincent, Prolog responds yes to the first query and no to the second.

However clause 1 does hold one small surprise for us. Consider the following query:

```
?- 'mia' = mia.
yes
```

What's going on here? Why do these two terms unify? Well, as far as Prolog is concerned, 'mia' and mia are the same atom. In fact, for Prolog, any atom of the form 'symbols' is considered the same entity as the atom of the form symbols. This can be a useful feature in certain kinds of programs, so don't forget it.

On the other hand, to the query

```
?- '2' = 2.
```

Prolog will respond no. And if you think about the definitions given in Chapter 1, you will see that this has to be the way things work. After all, 2 is a number, but '2' is an atom. They simply cannot be the same.

Let's try an example with a variable:

```
?- mia = X.

X = mia
yes
```

Again, this in an easy example: clearly the variable X can be unified with the constant mia, and Prolog does so, and tells us that it has made this unification. Fine, but how does this follow from our definition?

The relevant clause here is clause 2. This tells us what happens when at least one of the arguments is a variable. In our example it is the second term which is the variable. The definition tells us unification is possible, and also says that the variable is instantiated to the first argument, namely mia. And this, of course, is exactly what Prolog does.

Now for an important example: what happens with the following query?

```
?- X = Y.
```

Well, depending on your Prolog implementation, you may just get back the output

```
?- X = Y.
yes
```

Prolog is simply agreeing that the two terms unify (after all, variables unify with anything, so they certainly unify with each other) and making a note that from now on, X and Y denote the same object, that is, share values.

On the other hand, you may get the following output:

```
X = _5071
Y = _5071
yes
```

What's going on here? Essentially the same thing. Note that _5071 is a variable (recall from Chapter 1 that strings of letters and numbers that start with the underscore character are variables). Now look at clause 2 of the definition of unification. This tells us that when two variables are unified, they share values. So Prolog has created a new variable (namely _5071) and from now on both X and Y share the value of this variable. In effect, Prolog is creating a common variable name for the two original variables. Needless to say, there's nothing magic about the number 5071. Prolog just needs to generate a brand new variable name, and using numbers is a handy way to do this. It might just as well generate _5075, or _6189, or whatever.

Here is another example involving only atoms and variables. How do you think will Prolog respond?

```
?- X = mia, X = vincent.
```

Prolog will respond no. This query involves two goals, X = mia and
X = vincent. Taken separately, Prolog would succeed at both of them,
instantiating X to mia in the first case and to vincent in the second.
And that's exactly the problem here: once Prolog has worked through
the first goal, X is instantiated to (and therefore equal to) mia, so that it
simply can't unify with vincent anymore. Hence the second goal fails.
An *instantiated* variable isn't really a variable anymore: it has become
what it was instantiated with.

Now let's look at an example involving complex terms:

```
?- k(s(g),Y) = k(X,t(k)).

X = s(g)
Y = t(k)
yes
```

Clearly the two complex terms unify if the stated variable instantiations
are carried out. But how does this follow from the definition? Well,
first of all, clause 3 has to be used here because we are trying to
unify two complex terms. So the first thing we need to do is check
that both complex terms have the same functor and arity. And they
do. Clause 3 also tells us that we have to unify the corresponding
arguments in each complex term. So do the first arguments, s(g) and
X, unify? By clause 2, yes, and we instantiate X to s(g). So do the
second arguments, Y and t(k), unify? Again by clause 2, yes, and we
instantiate Y to t(k).

Here's another example with complex terms:

```
?- k(s(g), t(k)) = k(X,t(Y)).

X = s(g)
Y = k
yes
```

It should be clear that the two terms unify if these instantiations are
carried out. But can you explain, step by step, how this relates to the
definition?

Here is a last example:

```
?- loves(X,X) = loves(marcellus,mia).
```

Do these terms unify? No, they don't. It's true that they are both
complex terms and have the same functor and arity, but clause 3 also
demands that all corresponding arguments have to unify, and that the

variable instantiations have to be compatible. This is not the case here. Unifying the first arguments would instantiate X with marcellus. Unifying the second arguments would instantiate X with mia. Either way, we're blocked.

The occurs check

Unification is a well-known concept, used in several branches of computer science. It has been thoroughly studied, and many unification algorithms are known. But Prolog does *not* use a standard unification algorithm when it performs its version of unification. Instead it takes a shortcut. You need to know about this shortcut.

Consider the following query:

```
?- father(X) = X.
```

Do these terms unify or not? A standard unification algorithm would say: "No, they don't". Why is that? Well, pick any term and instantiate X to the term you picked. For example, if you instantiate X to father(father(butch)), the left hand side becomes father(father(father(butch))), and the right hand side becomes father(father(butch)). Obviously these don't unify. Moreover, it makes no difference what term you instantiate X to. No matter what you choose, the two terms cannot possibly be made the same, for the term on the left will always be one symbol longer than the term on the right (the functor father on the left will always give it that one extra level). A standard unification algorithm will spot this (we'll see why shortly when we discuss the occurs check), halt, and tell us no.

The recursive definition of Prolog unification given earlier won't do this. Because the left hand term is the variable X, by clause 2 it decides that the terms *do* unify, and (in accordance with clause 2) instantiates X to the right hand side, namely father(X). But there's an X in this term, and X has been instantiated to father(X), so Prolog realises that father(X) is really father(father(X)). But there's an X here too, and X has been instantiated to father(X), so Prolog realises that father(father(X)) is really father(father(father(X))), and so on. Having instantiated X to father(X), Prolog is committed to carrying out an unending sequence of expansions.

At least, that's the theory. What happens in practice? Well, with older Prolog implementations, what we've just described is exactly what happens. You would get a message like:

```
Not enough memory to complete query!
```

and a long string of symbols like:

```
X = father(father(father(father(father(father
    (father(father(father(father(father(father
    (father(father(father(father(father(father
    (father(father(father(father(father(father
    (father(father(father(father(father(father
```

Prolog is desperately *trying* to come back with the correctly instantiated terms, but it can't halt, because the instantiation process is unbounded. From an abstract mathematical perspective, what Prolog is trying to do is sensible. Intuitively, the only way the two terms could be made to unify would be if X was instantiated to a term containing an infinitely long string of `father` functors, so that the effect of the extra `father` functor on the left hand side was cancelled out. But the terms we compute with are *finite* entities. Infinite terms are an interesting mathematical abstraction, but they're not something we can work with. No matter how hard Prolog tries, it can never build one.

Now, it's annoying to have Prolog running out of memory like this, and sophisticated Prolog implementations have found ways of coping more gracefully. Try posing the query `father(X) = X` to SWI Prolog or SICStus Prolog. The answer will be something like:

```
X = father(father(father(father(...))))))))
yes
```

That is, these implementations insist that unification *is* possible, but they *don't* fall into the trap of actually trying to instantiate a finite term for X as the naive implementations do. Instead, they detect that there is a potential problem, halt, declare that unification is possible, and print out a finite representation of an infinite term, like the

```
father(father(father(father(...))))))))
```

in the previous query. Can you compute with these finite representations of infinite terms? That depends on the implementation. In some systems you cannot do much with them. For example, posing the query

```
?- X = father(X), Y = father(Y), X = Y.
```

would result in a crash (note that the X = Y demands that we unify two finite representations of infinite terms). Nonetheless, in some modern systems unification works robustly with such representations (for example, both SWI and Sicstus can handle the previous example) so you can actually use them in your programs. However, why you might want to use such representations, and what such representations actually are, are topics that lie beyond the scope of this book.

In short, there are actually *three* different responses to the question "does father(X) unify with X". There is the answer given by the standard unification algorithm (which is to say no), the response of older Prolog implementations (which is to run amok until they use up the available memory), and the answer given by sophisticated Prolog implementations (which is to say yes, and return a finite representation of an infinite term). In short, there is no 'right' answer to this question. What is important is that you understand the difference between standard unification and Prolog unification, and know how the Prolog implementation that you work with handles such examples.

Now, in the practical session at the end of the chapter we ask you to try out such examples with your Prolog interpreter. Here we want to say a little more about the difference between Prolog unification and standard unification. Given the very different ways they handle this example, it may seem that standard unification algorithms and the Prolog approach to unification are inherently different. Actually, they're not. There is one simple difference between the two algorithms that accounts for their different behaviour when faced with the task of unifying terms like X and father(X). A standard algorithm, when given two terms to unify, first carries out what is known as the occurs check. This means that if it is asked to unify a variable with a term, it first checks whether the variable occurs in the term. If it does, the standard algorithm declares that unification is impossible, for clearly it is the presence of the variable X in father(X) which leads to the problems discussed earlier. Only if the variable does not occur in the term do standard algorithms attempt to carry out the unification.

occurs check

To put it another way, standard unification algorithms are *pessimistic*. They first carry out the occurs check, and only when they are sure that the situation is safe they do go ahead and actually try to unify the terms. So a standard unification algorithm will never get locked into a situation where it is endlessly trying to instantiate variables, or having to appeal to infinite terms.

Prolog, on the other hand, is *optimistic*. It assumes that you are not going to give it anything dangerous. So it takes a shortcut: it omits the occurs check. As soon as you give it two terms, it rushes ahead and tries to unify them. As Prolog is a programming language, this is an intelligent strategy. Unification is one of the fundamental processes that makes Prolog work, so it needs to be carried out as fast as possible. Carrying out an occurs check every time unification is called for would slow it down considerably. Pessimism is safe, but optimism is a lot faster! Prolog can only run into problems if you, the programmer, ask it to do something like unify X with father(X). And it is unlikely you will ever (intentionally) ask it to do anything like that when writing a real program.

One final remark. Prolog comes with a built-in predicate that carries out standard unification (that is, unification with the occurs check). The predicate is

```
unify_with_occurs_check/2.
```

So if we posed the query

```
?- unify_with_occurs_check(father(X),X).
```

we would get the response no.

Programming with unification

As we've said, unification is a fundamental operation in Prolog. It plays a key role in Prolog proof search (as we shall soon learn), and this alone makes it vital. However, as you get to know Prolog better, it will become clear that unification is interesting and important in its own right. Indeed, sometimes you can write useful programs simply by using complex terms to define interesting concepts. Unification can then be used to pull out the information you want.

Here's a simple example of this, due to Ivan Bratko.[1] The following two line knowledge base defines two predicates, namely vertical/2 and horizontal/2, which specify what it means for a line to be vertical or horizontal respectively:

```
vertical(line(point(X,Y),point(X,Z))).
```

```
horizontal(line(point(X,Y),point(Z,Y))).
```

Now, at first glance this knowledge base may seem too simple to be interesting: it contains just two facts, and no rules. But wait a minute: the two facts are expressed using complex terms which again have complex terms as arguments. Indeed, there are three levels of terms nested inside terms. Moreover, the deepest level arguments are all variables, so the concepts are being defined in a general way. Maybe it's not quite as simple as it seems. Let's take a closer look.

Right down at the bottom level, we have a complex term with functor point and two arguments. Its two arguments are intended to be instantiated to numbers: point(X,Y) represents the Cartesian coordinates

---

[1]See his book *Prolog Programing for Artificial Intelligence*, Addison-Wesley Publishing Company, 1990, second edition, pages 41–43.

of a point. That is, the X indicates the horizontal distance the point is
from some fixed point, while the Y indicates the vertical distance from
that same fixed point.

Now, once we've specified two distinct points, we've specified a line,
namely the line between them. So the two complex terms representing
points are bundled together as the two arguments of another complex
term with the functor line. In effect, we represent a line by a complex
term which has two arguments which are complex terms themselves and
represent points. We're using Prolog's ability to build complex terms to
work our way up a hierarchy of concepts.

Being vertical, and being horizontal, are properties of lines. The
predicates vertical and horizontal therefore both take one argument
which represents a line. The definition of vertical/1 simply says: a
line that goes between two points that have the same x-coordinate is
vertical. Note how we capture the effect of "the same x-coordinate"
in Prolog: we simply make use of the same variable X as the first
argument of the two complex terms representing the points.

Similarly, the definition of horizontal/1 simply says: a line that
goes between two points that have the same y-coordinate is horizontal.
To capture the effect of "the same y-coordinate", we use the same
variable Y as the second argument of the two complex terms representing
the points.

What can we do with this knowledge base? Let's look at some
examples:

```
?- vertical(line(point(1,1),point(1,3))).
yes
```

This should be clear: the query unifies with the definition of vertical/1
in our little knowledge base (and in particular, the representations of the
two points have the same first argument) so Prolog says yes. Similarly
we have:

```
?- vertical(line(point(1,1),point(3,2))).
no
```

This query does not unify with the definition of vertical/1 (the
representations of the two points have different first arguments) so Prolog
says no.

But we can also ask more general questions:

```
?- horizontal(line(point(1,1),point(2,Y))).
```

```
Y = 1 ;

no
```

Here our query is: if we want a horizontal line between a point at
(1,1), and point whose x-coordinate is 2, what should the y-coordinate
of that second point be? Prolog correctly tells us that the y-coordinate
should be 1. If we then ask Prolog for a second possibility (note the ;)
it tells us that no other possibilities exist.

Now consider the following:

```
?- horizontal(line(point(2,3),P)).

P = point(_1972,3) ;

no
```

This query is: if we want a horizontal line between a point at (2,3),
and some other point, what other points are permissible? The answer
is: any point whose y-coordinate is 3. Note that the _1972 in the first
argument of the answer is a variable, which is Prolog's way of telling
us that any x-coordinate at all will do.

A general remark: the answer given to our last query, namely
point(_1972,3), is *structured*. That is, the answer is a complex
term, representing a sophisticated concept (namely "any point whose
y-coordinate is 3"). This structure was built using unification and nothing
else: no logical inference (and in particular, no use of modus ponens)
was used to produce it. Building structure by unification turns out to
be a powerful idea in Prolog programming, far more powerful than this
rather simple example might suggest. Moreover, when a program is
written that makes heavy use of unification, it is likely to be extremely
efficient. We will study a beautiful example in Chapter 7 when we
discuss difference lists, which are used to implement Prolog's built-in
grammar system, Definite Clause Grammars.

This style of programming is particularly useful in applications where
the important concepts have a natural hierarchical structure (as they did
in the simple knowledge base above), for we can then use complex
terms to represent this structure, and unification to access it. This
way of working plays an important role in computational linguistics, for
example, because information about language has a natural hierarchical
structure (think of the way sentences can be analysed into noun phrases
and verb phrases, and noun phrases analysed into determiners and nouns,
and so on).

2 Proof Search

Now that we know about unification, we are in a position to learn how
Prolog actually searches a knowledge base to see if a query is satisfied.
That is, we are ready to learn about proof search. We will introduce
the basic ideas involved by working through a simple example.

Suppose we are working with the following knowledge base

```
f(a).
f(b).

g(a).
g(b).

h(b).

k(X) :- f(X), g(X), h(X).
```

Suppose we then pose the query

```
?- k(Y).
```

It is probably clear that there is only one answer to this query, namely
k(b), but how exactly does Prolog work this out? Let's see.

Prolog reads the knowledge base, and tries to unify k(Y) with either
a fact, or the head of a rule. It searches the knowledge base top
to bottom, and carries out the unification, if it can, at the first place
possible. Here there is only one possibility: it must unify k(Y) to the
head of the rule k(X) :- f(X), g(X), h(X).

When Prolog unifies the variable in a query to a variable in a fact
or rule, it generates a brand new variable (say _G34) to represent the
shared variables. So the original query now reads:

```
k(_G34)
```

and Prolog knows that

```
k(_G34) :- f(_G34), g(_G34), h(_G34).
```

So what do we now have? The original query says: "I want to find
an individual that has property k". The rule says, "an individual has
property k if it has properties f, g, and h". So if Prolog can find an
individual with properties f, g, and h, it will have satisfied the original
query. So Prolog replaces the original query with the following list of
goals:

```
f(_G34), g(_G34), h(_G34).
```

Our discussion of the querying process so far can be made more elegant and succinct if we think graphically. Consider the following diagram:

```
                        ┌─────────┐
                        │ ?- k(Y) │
                        └────┬────┘
            Y = _G34         │
        ┌────────────────────┴────────────┐
        │ ?- f(_G34),g(_G34),h(_G34)       │
        └──────────────────────────────────┘
```

Everything in a box is either a query or a goal. In particular, our original goal was to prove k(Y), thus this is shown in the top box. When we unified k(Y) with the head of the rule in the knowledge base, X Y, and the new internal variable _G34 were made to share values, and we were left with the goals f(_G34),g(_G34),h(_G34), just as shown.

Now, whenever it has a list of goals, Prolog tries to satisfy them one by one, working through the list in a left to right direction. The leftmost goal is f(_G34), which reads: "I want an individual with property f". Can this goal be satisfied? Prolog tries to do so by searching through the knowledge base from top to bottom. The first item it finds that unifies with this goal is the fact f(a). This satisfies the goal f(_G34) and we are left with two more goals. Now, when we unify f(_G34) to f(a), _G34 is instantiated to a, and this instantiation applies to all occurrences of _G34 in the list of goals. So the list now looks like this:

```
g(a),h(a)
```

and our graphical representation of the proof search now looks like this:

```
                        ┌─────────┐
                        │ ?- k(Y) │
                        └────┬────┘
            Y = _G34         │
        ┌────────────────────┴────────────┐
        │ ?- f(_G34),g(_G34),h(_G34)       │
        └────────────────┬─────────────────┘
            _G34 = a      │
                  ┌───────┴──────┐
                  │ ?- g(a),h(a) │
                  └──────────────┘
```

But the fact g(a) is in the knowledge base, so the first goal we have to prove is satisfied too. So the goal list becomes

```
h(a)
```

and the graphical representation is now

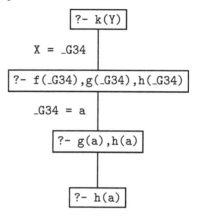

But there is no way to satisfy h(a), the last remaining goal. The only information about h we have in the knowledge base is h(b), and this won't unify with h(a).

So what happens next? Well, Prolog decides it has made a mistake, and checks whether it has missed any possible ways of unifying a goal with a fact or the head of a rule in the knowledge base. It does this by going back up the path shown in the graphical representation, looking for alternatives. Now, there is nothing else in the knowledge base that unifies with g(a), but there *is* another way of unifying f(_G34). Points in the search where there are several alternative ways of unifying a goal against the knowledge base are called choice points. Prolog keeps track of choice points it has encountered, so that if it makes a wrong choice it can retreat to the previous choice point and try something else instead. This process is called backtracking, and it is fundamental to proof search in Prolog.

So let's carry on with our example. Prolog backtracks to the last choice point. This is the point in the graphical representation where the list of goals was:

    f(_G34),g(_G34),h(_G34).

Prolog must now redo this work. First it must try to re-satisfy the first goal by searching further in the knowledge base. It can do this: it sees that it can unify the first goal with information in the knowledge base by unifying f(_G34) with f(b). This satisfies the goal f(_G34) and instantiates X to b, so that the remaining goal list is

    g(b),h(b).

But g(b) is a fact in the knowledge base, so this is satisfied too, leaving the goal list:

    h(b).

Moreover, this fact too is in the knowledge base, so this goal is also satisfied. So Prolog now has an empty list of goals. This means that it has now proved everything required to establish the original goal (that is, k(Y)). So the original query *is* satisfiable, and moreover, Prolog has also discovered what it has to do to satisfy it (namely instantiate Y to b).

It is interesting to consider what happens if we then ask for another solution by typing:

    ;

This forces Prolog to backtrack to the last choice point, to try and find another possibility. However, there are no other choice points, as there are no other possibilities for unifying h(b), g(b), f(_G34), or k(Y) with clauses in the knowledge base, so Prolog would respond no. On the other hand, if there had been other rules involving k, Prolog would have gone off and tried to use them in exactly the way we have described: that is, by searching top to bottom in the knowledge base, left to right in goal lists, and backtracking to the previous choice point whenever it fails.

Let's take a look at the graphical representation of the entire search process. Some general remarks are called for, for such representations are an important way of thinking about proof search in Prolog.

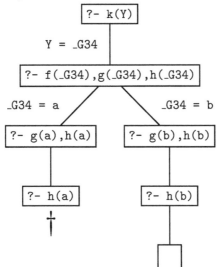

This diagram has the form of a tree; in fact it is our first example of
what is known as a search tree. The nodes of such trees say which
goals have to be satisfied at the various steps of the proof search, and
the edges keep track of the variable instantiations that are made when
the current goal (that is, the first one in the list of goals) is unified to
a fact or to the head of a rule in the knowledge base. Leaf nodes
which still contain unsatisfied goals are points where Prolog failed (either
because it made a wrong decision somewhere along the path, or because
no solution exists). Leaf nodes with an empty goal list correspond to
a possible solution. The edges along the path from the root node to a
successful leaf node tell you the variable instantiations that need to be
made to satisfy the original query.

Let's have a look at another example. Suppose that we are working
with the following knowledge base:

```
loves(vincent,mia).
loves(marcellus,mia).

jealous(A,B):- loves(A,C), loves(B,C).
```

Now we pose the query

```
?- jealous(X,Y).
```

The search tree for the query looks like this:

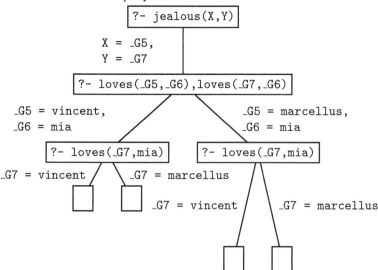

There is only one possible way of unifying jealous(X,Y) against
the knowledge base, namely by using the rule

```
jealous(A,B):- loves(A,C), loves(B,C).
```

So the new goals that have to be satisfied are:

```
loves(_G5,_G6),loves(_G7,_G6)
```

Now we have to unify `loves(_G5,_G6)` against the knowledge base. There are two ways of doing this (it can either be unified with the first fact or with the second fact) and this is why the path branches at this point. In both cases the goal `loves(_G7,mia)` remains, and this can also be satisfied by using either of two facts. All in all there are four leaf nodes with an empty goal list, which means that there are four ways of satisfying the original query. The variable instantiations for each solution can be read off the path from the root to the leaf node. So the four solutions are:

1. `X = _G5 = vincent and Y = _G7 = vincent`

2. `X = _G5 = vincent and Y = _G7 = marcellus`

3. `X = _G5 = marcellus and Y = _G7 = vincent`

4. `X = _G5 = marcellus and Y = _G7 = marcellus`

Work through his example carefully, and make sure you understand it.

3 Exercises

Exercise 2.1.   Which of the following pairs of terms unify? Where relevant, give the variable instantiations that lead to successful unification.

$\boxed{\mathcal{E}}$

1. `bread = bread`

2. `'Bread' = bread`

3. `'bread' = bread`

4. `Bread = bread`

5. `bread = sausage`

6. `food(bread) = bread`

7. `food(bread) = X`

8. `food(X) = food(bread)`

9. `food(bread,X) = food(Y,sausage)`

10. `food(bread,X,beer) = food(Y,sausage,X)`

11. `food(bread,X,beer) = food(Y,kahuna_burger)`

12. `food(X) = X`

13. `meal(food(bread),drink(beer)) = meal(X,Y)`

14. `meal(food(bread),X) = meal(X,drink(beer))`

Exercise 2.2.   We are working with the following knowledge base:

```
house_elf(dobby).
witch(hermione).
witch('McGonagall').
witch(rita_skeeter).
magic(X):- house_elf(X).
magic(X):- wizard(X).
magic(X):- witch(X).
```

Which of the following queries are satisfied? Where relevant, give all the variable instantiations that lead to success.

1. `?- magic(house_elf).`

2. `?- wizard(harry).`

3. `?- magic(wizard).`

4. `?- magic('McGonagall').`

5. `?- magic(Hermione).`

Draw the search tree for the query `magic(Hermione)`.

Exercise 2.3.   Here is a tiny lexicon (that is, information about individual words) and a mini grammar consisting of one syntactic rule (which defines a sentence to be an entity consisting of five words in the following order: a determiner, a noun, a verb, a determiner, a noun).

```
word(determiner,a).
word(determiner,every).
word(noun,criminal).
word(noun,'big kahuna burger').
word(verb,eats).
word(verb,likes).
```

```
sentence(Word1,Word2,Word3,Word4,Word5):-
  word(determiner,Word1),
  word(noun,Word2),
  word(verb,Word3),
  word(determiner,Word4),
  word(noun,Word5).
```

What query do you have to pose in order to find out which sentences the grammar can generate? List all sentences that this grammar can generate in the order that Prolog will generate them in.

Exercise 2.4. Here are six Italian words:

astante, astoria, baratto, cobalto, pistola, statale.

They are to be arranged, crossword puzzle fashion, in the following grid:

	V1	V2	V3
H1			
H2			
H3			

The following knowledge base represents a lexicon containing these words:

```
word(astante, a,s,t,a,n,t,e).
word(astoria, a,s,t,o,r,i,a).
word(baratto, b,a,r,a,t,t,o).
word(cobalto, c,o,b,a,l,t,o).
word(pistola, p,i,s,t,o,l,a).
word(statale, s,t,a,t,a,l,e).
```

Write a predicate crossword/6 that tells us how to fill in the grid. The first three arguments should be the vertical words from left to right, and the last three arguments the horizontal words from top to bottom.

4 Practical Session

By this stage, you should have had your first taste of running Prolog
programs. The purpose of the second practical session is to suggest two
sets of keyboard exercises which will help you get familiar with the
way Prolog works. The first set has to do with unification, the second
with proof search.

First of all, start up your Prolog interpreter. That is, get a screen
displaying the usual "I'm ready to start" prompt, which probably looks
something like:

    ?-

Verify your answers to Exercise 2.1, the unification examples. You don't
need to consult any knowledge bases, simply ask Prolog directly whether
it is possible to unify the terms by using the built-in =/2 predicate. For
example, to test whether food(bread,X) and food(Y,sausage) unify,
just type in

    food(bread,X) = food(Y,sausage).

and hit return.

You should also look at what happens when your Prolog implementation
attempts to unify terms that can't be unified because it doesn't carry out
an occurs check. For example, see what happens when you give it the
following query:

    g(X,Y) = Y.

If it handles such examples, try the trickier one mentioned in the text:

    X = f(X), Y = f(Y), X = Y.

Once you've experimented with that, it's time to move on to something
new. There is another built-in Prolog predicate for answering queries
about unification, namely \=/2 (that is: the 2-place predicate \=). This
works in the opposite way to the =/2 predicate: it succeeds when its
two arguments do *not* unify. For example, the terms a and b do not
unify, which explains the following dialogue:

    ?- a \= b.
    yes

Make sure you understand how \=/2 works by trying it out on (at
least) the following examples. But do this actively, not passively. That
is, after you type in an example, pause, and try to work out for yourself
what Prolog is going to respond. Only then hit return to see if you are
right.

1. a \= a

2. 'a' \= a

3. A \= a

4. f(a) \= a

5. f(a) \= A

6. f(A) \= f(a)

7. g(a,B,c) \= g(A,b,C)

8. g(a,b,c) \= g(A,C)

9. f(X) \= X

Thus the \=/2 predicate is (essentially) the negation of the =/2 predicate: a query involving one of these predicates will be satisfied when the corresponding query involving the other is not, and vice versa. This is the first example we have seen of a Prolog mechanism for handling negation. We discuss Prolog negation (and its peculiarities) in Chapter 10.

It's time to move on and introduce one of the most helpful tools in Prolog: trace. This is a built-in Prolog predicate that changes the way Prolog runs: it forces Prolog to evaluate queries one step at a time, indicating what it is doing at each step. Prolog waits for you to press return before it moves to the next step, so that you can see exactly what is going on. It was really designed to be used as a debugging tool, but it's also helpful when you're learning Prolog: stepping through programs using trace is an *excellent* way of learning how Prolog proof search works.

Let's look at an example. In the text, we looked at the proof search involved when we made the query k(Y) to the following knowledge base:

```
f(a).
f(b).

g(a).
g(b).

h(b).

k(X):- f(X), g(X), h(X).
```

Suppose this knowledge base is in file proof.pl. We first consult it:

```
?- [proof].
yes
```

We then type trace, followed by a full stop, and hit return:

```
?- trace.
yes
```

trace mode Prolog is now in trace mode, and will evaluate all queries step by step. For example, if we pose the query k(X), and then hit return every time Prolog comes back with a ?, we obtain (something like) the following:

```
[trace] 2 ?- k(X).
   Call: (6) k(_G34) ?
   Call: (7) f(_G34) ?
   Exit: (7) f(a) ?
   Call: (7) g(a) ?
   Exit: (7) g(a) ?
   Call: (7) h(a) ?
   Fail: (7) h(a) ?
   Fail: (7) g(a) ?
   Redo: (7) f(_G34) ?
   Exit: (7) f(b) ?
   Call: (7) g(b) ?
   Exit: (7) g(b) ?
   Call: (7) h(b) ?
   Exit: (7) h(b) ?
   Exit: (6) k(b) ?

X = b
yes
```

Study this carefully. That is, try doing the same thing yourself, and relate this output to the discussion of the example in the text, and in particular, to the nodes in the search tree. To get you started, we'll remark that the third line is where the variable in the query is (wrongly) instantiated to a. The first line marked fail is where Prolog realises it's taken the wrong path and starts to backtrack, and the line marked redo is where it tries alternatives for the goal f(_G34).

While learning Prolog, use trace, and use it heavily. It's a great way
to learn. Oh yes: you also need to know how to turn trace off. Simply
type notrace (followed by a full stop) and hit return:

```
?- notrace.
yes
```

Chapter 3

Recursion

This chapter has two main goals:

1. To introduce recursive definitions in Prolog.

2. To show that there can be mismatches between the declarative meaning of a Prolog program, and its procedural meaning.

1   Recursive Definitions

Predicates can be defined recursively. Roughly speaking, a predicate is recursively defined if one or more rules in its definition refers to itself.

Example 1: Eating

Consider the following knowledge base:

```
is_digesting(X,Y) :- just_ate(X,Y).
is_digesting(X,Y) :-
        just_ate(X,Z),
        is_digesting(Z,Y).

just_ate(mosquito,blood(john)).
just_ate(frog,mosquito).
just_ate(stork,frog).
```

At first glance this seems pretty ordinary: it's just a knowledge base containing three facts and two rules. But the definition of the is_digesting/2 predicate is recursive. Note that is_digesting/2 is (at least partially) defined in terms of itself, for the is_digesting/2 functor occurs in both the head and body of the second rule. Crucially, however, there is an 'escape' from this circularity. This is provided by the just_ate/2 predicate, which occurs in the first rule. (Significantly, the body of the first rule makes no mention of is_digesting/2.) Let's now consider both the declarative and procedural meanings of this definition.

The word "declarative" is used to talk about the logical meaning of Prolog knowledge bases. That is, the declarative meaning of a Prolog knowledge base is simply "what it says", or "what it means, if we read it as a collection of logical statements". And the declarative meaning of this recursive definition is fairly straightforward. The first clause (the escape clause, the one that is not recursive, or as we shall usually call it, the base clause), simply says that: *if* X has just eaten Y, *then* X is now digesting Y. This is obviously a sensible definition.

So what about the second clause, the recursive clause? This says that: *if* X has just eaten Z *and* Z is digesting Y, *then* X is digesting Y, too. Again, this is obviously a sensible definition.

So now we know what this recursive definition says, but what happens when we pose a query that actually needs to use this definition? That is, what does this definition actually do? To use the normal Prolog terminology, what is its procedural meaning?

recursive

declarative

procedural

base clause

recursive clause

This is also reasonably straightforward. The base rule is like all the earlier rules we've seen. That is, if we ask whether X is digesting Y, Prolog can use this rule to ask instead the question: has X just eaten Y?

What about the recursive clause? This gives Prolog another strategy for determining whether X is digesting Y: *it can try to find some* Z *such that* X *has just eaten* Z, *and* Z *is digesting* Y. That is, this rule lets Prolog break the task apart into two subtasks. Hopefully, doing so will eventually lead to simple problems which can be solved by simply looking up the answers in the knowledge base. The following picture sums up the situation:

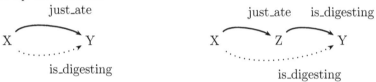

Let's see how this works. If we pose the query:

```
?- is_digesting(stork,mosquito).
```

then Prolog goes to work as follows. First, it tries to make use of the first rule listed concerning `is_digesting`; that is, the base rule. This tells it that X is digesting Y if X just ate Y, By unifying X with `stork` and Y with `mosquito` it obtains the following goal:

```
just_ate(stork,mosquito).
```

But the knowledge base doesn't contain the information that the stork just ate the mosquito, so this attempt fails. So Prolog next tries to make use of the second rule. By unifying X with `stork` and Y with `mosquito` it obtains the following goals:

```
just_ate(stork,Z),
is_digesting(Z,mosquito).
```

That is, to show `is_digesting(stork,mosquito)`, Prolog needs to find a value for Z such that, firstly,

```
just_ate(stork,Z).
```

and secondly,

```
is_digesting(Z,mosquito).
```

And there *is* such a value for Z, namely `frog`. It is immediate that

```
just_ate(stork,frog).
```

will succeed, for this fact is listed in the knowledge base. And deducing

```
is_digesting(frog,mosquito).
```

is almost as simple, for the first clause of is_digesting/2 reduces this goal to deducing

```
just_ate(frog,mosquito).
```

and this is a fact listed in the knowledge base.

Well, that's our first example of a recursive rule definition. We're going to learn a lot more about them, but one very practical remark should be made right away. Hopefully it's clear that when you write a recursive predicate, it should always have at least two clauses: a base clause (the clause that stops the recursion at some point), and one that contains the recursion. If you don't do this, Prolog can spiral off into an unending sequence of useless computations. For example, here's an extremely simple example of a recursive rule definition:

```
p :- p.
```

That's it. Nothing else. It's beautiful in its simplicity. And from a declarative perspective it's an extremely sensible (if rather boring) definition: it says "if property p holds, then property p holds". You can't argue with that.

But from a procedural perspective, this is a wildly dangerous rule. In fact, we have here the ultimate in dangerous recursive rules: exactly the same thing on both sides, and no base clause to let us escape. For consider what happens when we pose the following query:

```
?- p.
```

Prolog asks itself: "How do I prove p?" and it realises, "Hey, I've got a rule for that! To prove p I just need to prove p!". So it asks itself (again): "How do I prove p?" and it realises, "Hey, I've got a rule for that! To prove p I just need to prove p!". So it asks itself (yet again): "How do I prove p?" and it realises, "Hey, I've got a rule for that! To prove p I just need to prove p!" and so on and so forth.

If you make this query, Prolog won't answer you: it will head off, looping desperately away in an unending search. That is, it won't terminate, and you'll have to interrupt it. Of course, if you use trace, you can step through one step at a time, until you get sick of watching Prolog loop.

Example 2: Descendant

Now that we know something about *what* recursion in Prolog involves, it is time to ask *why* it is so important. Actually, this is a question that can be answered on a number of levels, but for now, let's keep things fairly practical. So: when it comes to writing useful Prolog programs, are recursive definitions really so important? And if so, why?

Let's consider an example. Suppose we have a knowledge base recording facts about the child relation:

```
child(bridget,caroline).
child(caroline,donna).
```

That is, Caroline is a child of Bridget, and Donna is a child of Caroline. Now suppose we wished to define the descendant relation; that is, the relation of being a child of, or a child of a child of, or a child of a child of a child of, and so on. Here's a first attempt to do this. We could add the following two *non*-recursive rules to the knowledge base:

```
descend(X,Y) :- child(X,Y).

descend(X,Y) :- child(X,Z),
                child(Z,Y).
```

Now, fairly obviously these definitions work up to a point, but they are clearly limited: they only define the concept of descendant-of for two generations or less. That's ok for the above knowledge base, but suppose we get some more information about the child-of relation and we expand our list of child-of facts to this:

```
child(anne,bridget).
child(bridget,caroline).
child(caroline,donna).
child(donna,emily).
```

Now our two rules are inadequate. For example, if we pose the queries

```
?- descend(anne,donna).
```

or

```
?- descend(bridget,emily).
```

we get the answer no, which is *not* what we want. Sure, we could 'fix' this by adding the following two rules:

```
descend(X,Y) :- child(X,Z_1),
                child(Z_1,Z_2),
                child(Z_2,Y).

descend(X,Y) :- child(X,Z_1),
                child(Z_1,Z_2),
                child(Z_2,Z_3),
                child(Z_3,Y).
```

But, let's face it, this is clumsy and hard to read. Moreover, if we add further child-of facts, we could easily find ourselves having to add more and more rules as our list of child-of facts grow, rules like:

```
descend(X,Y) :- child(X,Z_1),
                child(Z_1,Z_2),
                child(Z_2,Z_3),

                      .

                      .

                      .

                child(Z_17,Z_18).
                child(Z_18,Z_19).
                child(Z_19,Y).
```

This is not a particularly pleasant (or sensible) way to go!

But we don't need to do this at all. We can avoid having to use ever longer rules entirely. The following recursive predicate definition fixes everything exactly the way we want:

```
descend(X,Y) :- child(X,Y).

descend(X,Y) :- child(X,Z),
                descend(Z,Y).
```

What does this say? The declarative meaning of the base clause is: *if* Y is a child of X, *then* Y is a descendant of X. Obviously sensible. So what about the recursive clause? Its declarative meaning is: *if* Z is a child of X, *and* Y is a descendant of Z, *then* Y is a descendant of X. Again, this is obviously true.

So let's now look at the procedural meaning of this recursive predicate, by stepping through an example. What happens when we pose the query:

```
descend(anne,donna)
```

Prolog first tries the first rule. The variable X in the head of the rule is unified with anne and Y with donna and the next goal Prolog tries to prove is

```
child(anne,donna)
```

This attempt fails, however, since the knowledge base neither contains the fact `child(anne,donna)` nor any rules that would allow to infer it. So Prolog backtracks and looks for an alternative way of proving `descend(anne,donna)`. It finds the second rule in the knowledge base and now has the following subgoals:

```
child(anne,_633),
descend(_633,donna).
```

Prolog takes the first subgoal and tries to unify it with something in the knowledge base. It finds the fact `child(anne,bridget)` and the variable `_633` gets instantiated to `bridget`. Now that the first subgoal is satisfied, Prolog moves to the second subgoal. It has to prove

```
descend(bridget,donna)
```

This is the first recursive call of the predicate `descend/2`. As before, Prolog starts with the first rule, but fails, because the goal

```
child(bridget,donna)
```

cannot be proved. Backtracking, Prolog finds that there is a second possibility to be checked for `descend(bridget,donna)`, namely the second rule, which again gives Prolog two new subgoals:

```
child(bridget,_1785),
descend(_1785,donna).
```

The first one can be unified with the fact `child(bridget,caroline)` of the knowledge base, so that the variable `_1785` is instantiated with `caroline`. Next Prolog tries to prove

```
descend(caroline,donna).
```

This is the second recursive call of predicate `descend/2`. As before, it tries the first rule first, obtaining the following new goal:

```
child(caroline,donna)
```

This time Prolog succeeds, since `child(caroline,donna)` is a fact in the database. Prolog has found a proof for the goal `descend(caroline,donna)` (the second recursive call). But this means that `descend(bridget,donna)` (the first recursive call) is also true, which means that our original query `descend(anne,donna)` is true as well.

Here is the search tree for the query descend(anne,donna). Make
sure that you understand how it relates to the discussion in the text; that
is, how Prolog traverses this search tree when trying to prove this query.

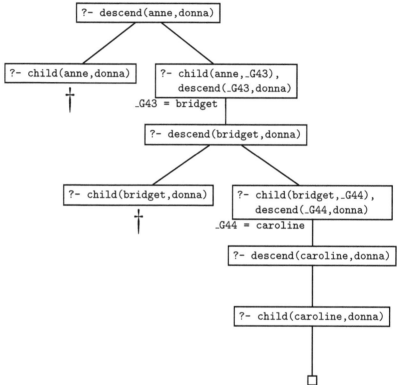

It should be obvious from this example that no matter how many
generations of children we add, we will always be able to work out the
descendant relation. That is, the recursive definition is both general and
compact: it contains *all* the information in the non-recursive rules, and
much more besides. The non-recursive rules only defined the descendant
concept up to some fixed number of generations: we would need to write
down infinitely many non-recursive rules if we wanted to capture this
concept fully, and of course that's impossible. But, in effect, that's what
the recursive rule does for us: it bundles up the information needed to
cope with arbitrary numbers of generations into just three lines of code.

Recursive rules are really important. They enable to pack an enormous
amount of information into a compact form and to define predicates in
a natural way. Most of the work you will do as a Prolog programmer
will involve writing recursive rules.

Example 3: Successor

In the previous chapter we remarked that building structure through unification is a key idea in Prolog programming. Now that we know about recursion, we can give more interesting illustrations of this.

Nowadays, when human beings write numerals, they usually use *decimal* notation (0, 1, 2, 3, 4, 5, 6, 7, 8, 9, 10, 11, 12, and so on) but as you probably know, there are many other notations. For example, because computer hardware is generally based on digital circuits, computers usually use *binary* notation to represent numerals (0, 1, 10, 11, 100, 101, 110, 111, 1000, and so on), for the 0 can be implemented as a switch being off, the 1 as a switch being on. Other cultures use different systems. For example, the ancient Babylonians used a base 60 system, while the ancient Romans used a rather ad-hoc system (I, II, III, IV, V, VI, VII, VIII, IX, X). This last example shows that notational issues can be important. If you don't believe this, try figuring out a systematic way of doing long-division in Roman notation. As you'll discover, it's a frustrating task. Apparently the Romans had a group of professionals (analogs of modern accountants) who specialised in this.

Well, here's yet another way of writing numerals, which is sometimes used in mathematical logic. It makes use of just four symbols: 0, *succ*, and the left and right parentheses. This style of numeral is defined by the following inductive definition:

1. 0 is a numeral.

2. If X is a numeral, then so is *succ(X)*.

As is probably clear, *succ* can be read as short for *successor*. That is, *succ(X)* represents the number obtained by adding one to the number represented by X. So this is a very simple notation: it simply says that 0 is a numeral, and that all other numerals are built by stacking *succ* symbols in front. (In fact, it's used in mathematical logic because of this simplicity. Although it wouldn't be pleasant to do household accounts in this notation, it is a very easy notation to prove things *about*.)

Now, by this stage it should be clear that we can turn this definition into a Prolog program. The following knowledge base does this:

```
numeral(0).

numeral(succ(X)) :- numeral(X).
```

So if we pose queries like

```
numeral(succ(succ(succ(0)))).
```

we get the answer yes.

But we can do some more interesting things. Consider what happens when we pose the following query:

```
numeral(X).
```

That is, we're saying "Ok, show me some numerals". Then we can have the following dialogue with Prolog:

```
X = 0 ;

X = succ(0) ;

X = succ(succ(0)) ;

X = succ(succ(succ(0))) ;

X = succ(succ(succ(succ(0)))) ;

X = succ(succ(succ(succ(succ(0))))) ;

X = succ(succ(succ(succ(succ(succ(0)))))) ;

X = succ(succ(succ(succ(succ(succ(succ(0))))))) ;

X = succ(succ(succ(succ(succ(succ(succ(succ(0))))))))
yes
```

Yes, Prolog is counting: but what's really important is *how* it's doing this. Quite simply, it's backtracking through the recursive definition, and actually *building* numerals using unification. This is an instructive example, and it is important that you understand it. The best way to do so is to sit down and try it out, with `trace` turned on.

Building and binding. Recursion, unification, and proof search. These are ideas that lie at the heart of Prolog programming. Whenever we have to generate or analyse recursively structured objects (such as these numerals) the interplay of these ideas makes Prolog a powerful

lists

tool. For example, in the next chapter we shall introduce lists, an extremely important recursive data structure, and we will see that Prolog is a natural list processing language. Many applications (computational linguistics is a prime example) make heavy use of recursively structured objects, such as trees and feature structures. So it's not particularly surprising that Prolog has proved useful in such applications.

Example 4: Addition

As a final example, let's see whether we can use the representation of numerals that we introduced in the previous section for doing simple arithmetic. Let's try to define addition. That is, we want to define a predicate add/3 which when given two numerals as the first and second argument returns the result of adding them up as its third argument. For example:

```
?- add(succ(succ(0)),succ(succ(0)),
       succ(succ(succ(succ(0))))).
yes
?- add(succ(succ(0)),succ(0),Y).
Y = succ(succ(succ(0)))
```

There are two things which are important to notice:

1. Whenever the first argument is 0, the third argument has to be the same as the second argument:

```
?- add(0,succ(succ(0)),Y).
Y = succ(succ(0))
?- add(0,0,Y).
Y = 0
```

This is the case that we want to use for the base clause.

2. Assume that we want to add the two numerals X and Y (for example succ(succ(succ(0))) and succ(succ(0))) and that X is not 0. Now, if X1 is the numeral that has one succ functor less than X (that is, succ(succ(0)) in our example) and if we know the result – let's call it Z – of adding X1 and Y (namely succ(succ(succ(succ(0))))), then it is very easy to compute the result of adding X and Y: we just have to add one succ-functor to Z. This is what we want to express with the recursive clause.

Here is the predicate definition that expresses exactly what we just said:

```
add(0,Y,Y).
add(succ(X),Y,succ(Z)) :-
        add(X,Y,Z).
```

So what happens, if we give Prolog this predicate definition and then ask:

```
?- add(succ(succ(succ(0))), succ(succ(0)), R).
```

Let's go step by step through the way Prolog processes this query. The trace and search tree for the query are given below.

The first argument is not 0, which means that only the second clause for add/3 can be used. This leads to a recursive call of add/3. The outermost succ functor is stripped off the first argument of the original query, and the result becomes the first argument of the recursive query. The second argument is passed on unchanged to the recursive query, and the third argument of the recursive query is a variable, the internal variable _G648 in the trace given below. Note that _G648 is not instantiated yet. However it shares values with R (the variable that we used as the third argument in the original query) because R was instantiated to succ(_G648) when the query was unified with the head of the second clause. But that means that R is not a completely uninstantiated variable anymore. It is now a complex term, that has a (uninstantiated) variable as its argument.

The next two steps are essentially the same. With every step the first argument becomes one layer of succ smaller; both the trace and the search tree given below show this nicely. At the same time, a succ functor is added to R at every step, but always leaving the innermost variable uninstantiated. After the first recursive call R is succ(_G648). After the second recursive call, _G648 is instantiated with succ(_G650), so that R is succ(succ(_G650). After the third recursive call, _G650 is instantiated with succ(_G652) and R therefore becomes succ(succ(succ(_G652))). The search tree shows this step by step instantiation.

At this stage all succ functors have been stripped off the first argument and we can apply the base clause. The third argument is equated with the second argument, so the 'hole' (the uninstantiated variable) in the complex term R is finally filled, and we are through.

Here's the complete trace of our query:

```
Call: (6) add(succ(succ(succ(0))), succ(succ(0)), R)

Call: (7) add(succ(succ(0)), succ(succ(0)), _G648)

Call: (8) add(succ(0), succ(succ(0)), _G650)

Call: (9) add(0, succ(succ(0)), _G652)
```

Exit: (9) add(0, succ(succ(0)), succ(succ(0)))

Exit: (8) add(succ(0), succ(succ(0)), succ(succ(succ(0))))

Exit: (7) add(succ(succ(0)), succ(succ(0)),
                                    succ(succ(succ(succ(0)))))

Exit: (6) add(succ(succ(succ(0))), succ(succ(0)),
                              succ(succ(succ(succ(succ(0))))))

And here's the search tree:

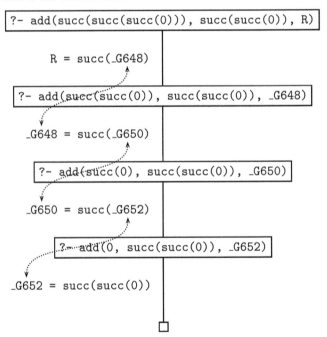

2 Rule Ordering, Goal Ordering, and Termination

Prolog was the first reasonably successful attempt to create a logic programming language. Underlying logic programming is a simple (and seductive) vision: the task of the programmer is simply to *describe* problems. The programmer should write down (in the language of logic) a declarative specification (that is: a knowledge base), which describes the situation of interest. The programmer shouldn't have to tell the computer *what* to do. To get information, he or she simply asks the

logic pro-
gramming

questions. It's up to the logic programming system to figure out how to get the answer.

Well, that's the idea, and it should be clear that Prolog has taken some important steps in this direction. But Prolog is *not*, repeat *not*, a full logic programming language. If you only think about the declarative meaning of a Prolog program, you are in for a very tough time. As we learned in the previous chapter, Prolog has a very specific way of working out the answers to queries: it searches the knowledge base from top to bottom, clauses from left to right, and uses backtracking to recover from bad choices. These procedural aspects have an important influence on what actually happens when you make a query. We have already seen a dramatic example of a mismatch between the procedural and declarative meaning of a knowledge base (remember the p:- p program?), and as we shall now see, it is easy to define knowledge bases which (read logically) describe the same situations, but which behave very differently. Let's consider the matter.

Recall our earlier descendant program (let's call it descend1.pl):

```
child(anne,bridget).
child(bridget,caroline).
child(caroline,donna).
child(donna,emily).

descend(X,Y) :- child(X,Y).

descend(X,Y) :- child(X,Z),
                descend(Z,Y).
```

We'll make one change to it, and call the result descend2.pl:

```
child(anne,bridget).
child(bridget,caroline).
child(caroline,donna).
child(donna,emily).

descend(X,Y) :- child(X,Z),
                descend(Z,Y).

descend(X,Y) :- child(X,Y).
```

rule order   All we have done is change the rule order. So if we read the program as a purely logical definition, nothing has changed. But does the change give rise to procedural differences? Yes, but nothing significant. For

example, if you work through the examples you will see that the first
solution that descend1.pl finds is

```
X = anne
Y = bridget
```

whereas the first solution that descend2.pl finds is

```
X = anne
Y = emily
```

But (as you should check) both programs generate exactly the same
answers, they merely find them in a different order. And this is a
general point. Roughly speaking (we'll add a caveat later on) changing
the order of rules in a Prolog program does not change (up to the order
in which solutions are found) the program's behaviour.

So let's move on. We'll make one small change to descend2.pl,
and call the result descend3.pl:

```
child(anne,bridget).
child(bridget,caroline).
child(caroline,donna).
child(donna,emily).

descend(X,Y) :- descend(Z,Y),
                child(X,Z).

descend(X,Y) :- child(X,Y).
```

Note the difference. Here we've changed the goal order *within* a rule,
not the rule order. Now, once again, if we read the program as a
purely logical definition, nothing has changed; it means the same thing
as the previous two versions. But this time the program's behaviour has
changed dramatically. For example, if you pose the query

```
descend(anne,emily).
```

goal order

you will get an error message ("out of local stack", or something
similar). Prolog is looping. Why? Well, in order to satisfy the query
descend(anne,emily) Prolog uses the first rule. This means that its
next goal will be to satisfy the query

```
descend(W1,emily)
```

for some new variable W1. But to satisfy this new goal, Prolog again
has to use the first rule, and this means that its next goal is going to be

```
descend(W2,emily)
```

for some new variable W2. And of course, this in turn means that its next
goal is going to be descend(W3,emily) and then descend(W4,emily),
and so on. That is, the (at first glance innocuous) change in the goal
order has resulted in procedural disaster. To use the standard terminology,
we have here a classic example of a left recursive rule, that is, a rule
where the leftmost item of the body is identical (modulo the choice of
variables) with the rule's head. As our example shows, such rules easily
give rise to non-terminating computations. Goal order, and in particular
left recursion, is the root of all evil when it comes to non-termination.

left
recursive
rule

Still, as we said earlier, we need to make one small caveat about
rule ordering. We said earlier that rule ordering only changes the order
in which solutions are found. However this may not be true if we are
working with non-terminating programs. To see this, consider the fourth
(and last) variant of our descendant program, namely descend4.pl:

```
child(anne,bridget).
child(bridget,caroline).
child(caroline,donna).
child(donna,emily).

descend(X,Y) :- child(X,Y).

descend(X,Y) :- descend(Z,Y),
                child(X,Z).
```

This program is descend3.pl with the rule ordering reversed. Now
(once again) this program has the same declarative meaning as the other
variants, but it is also procedurally different from its relatives. First, and
most obviously, it is very different procedurally from both descend1.pl
and descend2.pl. In particular, because it contains a left recursive rule,
this new program does not terminate on some input. For example (just
like descend3.pl) this new program does not terminate when we pose
the query

```
descend(anne,emily).
```

But descend4.pl is not procedurally identical to descend3.pl. The
rule ordering reversal does make a difference. For example, descend3.pl
will not terminate if we pose the query

```
descend(anne,bridget).
```

However `descend4.pl` will terminate in this case, for the rule reversal enables it to apply the non-recursive rule and halt. So when it comes to non-terminating programs, rule ordering changes can lead to some extra solutions being found. Nonetheless, goal ordering, not rule ordering, is what is truly procedurally significant. To ensure termination, we need to pay attention to the order of goals within the bodies of rules. Tinkering with rule orderings does not get to grips with the roots of termination problems — at best it can yield some extra solutions.

Summing up, our four variant descendant programs are Prolog knowledge bases which describe exactly the same situations, but behave differently. The difference in behaviour between `descend1.pl` and `descend2.pl` (which differ only in the way rules are ordered) is relatively minor: they generate the same solutions, but in a different order. But `descend3.pl` and `descend4.pl` are procedurally very different from their two cousins, and this is because they differ from them in the way their goals are ordered. In particular, both these variants contain left recursive rules, and in both cases this leads to non-terminating behaviour. The change in rule ordering between `descend3.pl` and `descend4.pl` merely means that `descend4.pl` will terminate in some cases where `descend3.pl` will not.

What are the ramifications of our discussion for the practicalities of producing working Prolog programs? It's probably best to say the following. Often you can get the overall idea (the big picture) of how to write the program by thinking declaratively, that is, by thinking in terms of describing the problem accurately. This is an excellent way to approach problems, and certainly the one most in keeping with the spirit of logic programming. But once you've done that, you need to think about how Prolog will work with knowledge bases you have written. In particular, to ensure termination, you need to check that the goal orderings you have given are sensible. The basic rule of thumb is never to write as the leftmost goal of the body something that is identical (modulo variable names) with the goal given in the head. Rather, place such goals (which trigger recursive calls) as far as possible towards the right of the tail. That is, place them after the goals which test for the various (non-recursive) termination conditions. Doing this gives Prolog a sporting chance of fighting it's way through your recursive definitions to find solutions.

3   Exercises

Exercise 3.1.   In the text, we discussed the predicate

```
descend(X,Y) :- child(X,Y).
descend(X,Y) :- child(X,Z),
                descend(Z,Y).
```

Suppose we reformulated this predicate as follows:

```
descend(X,Y) :- child(X,Y).
descend(X,Y) :- descend(X,Z),
                descend(Z,Y).
```

Would this be problematic?

Exercise 3.2.   Do you know these wooden Russian dolls (Matryoshka dolls) where the smaller ones are contained in bigger ones? Here is a schematic picture:

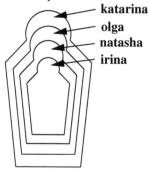

First, write a knowledge base using the predicate `directlyIn/2` which encodes which doll is directly contained in which other doll. Then, define a recursive predicate `in/2`, that tells us which doll is (directly or indirectly) contained in which other dolls. For example, the query `in(katarina,natasha)` should evaluate to true, while `in(olga, katarina)` should fail.

Exercise 3.3.   We have the following knowledge base:

```
directTrain(saarbruecken,dudweiler).
directTrain(forbach,saarbruecken).
directTrain(freyming,forbach).
directTrain(stAvold,freyming).
directTrain(fahlquemont,stAvold).
directTrain(metz,fahlquemont).
directTrain(nancy,metz).
```

That is, this knowledge base holds facts about towns it is possible to travel between by taking a *direct* train. But of course, we can travel further by chaining together direct train journeys. Write a recursive predicate `travelFromTo/2` that tells us when we can travel by train between two towns. For example, when given the query

```
travelFromTo(nancy,saarbruecken).
```

it should reply yes.

Exercise 3.4. Define a predicate `greater_than/2` that takes two numerals in the notation that we introduced in the text (that is, 0, succ(0), succ(succ(0)), and so on) as arguments and decides whether the first one is greater than the second one. For example:

```
?- greater_than(succ(succ(succ(0))),succ(0)).
yes
?- greater_than(succ(succ(0)),succ(succ(succ(0)))).
no
```

Exercise 3.5. Binary trees are trees where all internal nodes have exactly two children. The smallest binary trees consist of only one leaf node. We will represent leaf nodes as `leaf(Label)`. For instance, `leaf(3)` and `leaf(7)` are leaf nodes, and therefore small binary trees. Given two binary trees B1 and B2 we can combine them into one binary tree using a predicate `tree/2` as follows: `tree(B1,B2)`. So, from the leaves `leaf(1)` and `leaf(2)` we can build the binary tree `tree(leaf(1),leaf(2))`. And from the binary trees `tree(leaf(1),leaf(2))` and `leaf(4)` we can build the binary tree `tree(tree(leaf(1), leaf(2)),leaf(4))`.

Now, define a predicate `swap/2`, which produces the mirror image of the binary tree that is its first argument. For example:

```
?- swap(tree(tree(leaf(1), leaf(2)), leaf(4)),T).
T = tree(leaf(4), tree(leaf(2), leaf(1))).
yes
```

4 Practical Session

By now, you should feel more at home with writing and running basic Prolog programs. In this practical session we first suggest two series of keyboard exercises which will help you get familiar with recursive definitions in Prolog, and then give you some programming problems to solve.

First the keyboard exercises. As recursive programming is so fundamental to Prolog, it is important that you have a firm grasp of what it involves. In particular, it is important that you understand the process of variable instantiation when recursive definitions are used, and that you understand why the order of goals in rules can make the difference between termination and non-termination. So:

1. Load `descend1.pl`, turn on `trace`, and pose the query `descend(anne,emily)`. Count how many steps it takes Prolog to work out the answer (that is, how many times do you have to hit the return key). Now turn `trace` off and pose the query `descend(X,Y)`. How many answers are there?

2. Load `descend2.pl`. This is the variant of `descend1.pl` with the rule order reversed. Repeat the traces you have carried out for `descend1.pl`, and compare the results.

3. Load `descend3.pl`. This is the variant of `descend2.pl` in which the goal order within the recursive rule is switched, resulting in a left recursive rule. Because of this, even for such simple queries as `descend(anne,bridget)`, Prolog will not terminate. Step through an example, using `trace`, to confirm this.

4. Load `descend4.pl`. This is the variant of `descend3.pl` obtained by switching the rule order. So `descend4.pl` also contains a left recursive rule, and does not terminate on all input. But it does terminate on some input where `descend3.pl` does not. Which extra solutions does it find?

As we said in the text, goal ordering, not rule ordering is what is truly procedurally significant. But with non-terminating programs, rule ordering changes can have unexpected effects. Recall the successor program discussed in the text (let's call it `numeral1.pl`):

```
numeral(0).
numeral(succ(X)) :- numeral(X).
```

Let's swap the order of the two clauses, and call the result `numeral2.pl`:

```
numeral(succ(X)) :- numeral(X).
numeral(0).
```

Clearly the declarative, or logical, content of this program is exactly the same as the earlier version. But what are the procedural differences, if any?

1. Create a file containing `numeral2.pl`, load it, and investigate what happens if we pose queries about *specific* numerals. For example, suppose we ask:

   ```
   numeral(succ(succ(succ(0)))).
   ```

   Do `numeral1.pl` and `numeral2.pl` behave in the same way on such input?

2. Second, look at what happens if we try to *generate* numerals, that is, suppose we pose the query

   ```
   numeral(X).
   ```

   Do the programs display identical behaviour?

Here are some programs for you to try your hand at.

1. Imagine that the following knowledge base describes a maze. The facts determine which points are connected, that is, from which points you can get to which other points in one step. Furthermore, imagine that all paths are one-way streets, so that you can only walk them in one direction. So, you can get from point 1 to point 2, but not the other way round.

   ```
   connected(1,2).
   connected(3,4).
   connected(5,6).
   connected(7,8).
   connected(9,10).
   connected(12,13).
   connected(13,14).
   connected(15,16).
   connected(17,18).
   connected(19,20).
   connected(4,1).
   connected(6,3).
   connected(4,7).
   connected(6,11).
   connected(14,9).
   connected(11,15).
   connected(16,12).
   connected(14,17).
   connected(16,19).
   ```

Write a predicate path/2 that tells you from which points in the maze you can get to which other points when chaining together connections given in the above knowledge base. Can you get from point 5 to point 10? Which other point can you get to when starting at point 1? And which points can be reached from point 13?

2. We are given the following knowledge base of travel information:

```
byCar(auckland,hamilton).
byCar(hamilton,raglan).
byCar(valmont,saarbruecken).
byCar(valmont,metz).

byTrain(metz,frankfurt).
byTrain(saarbruecken,frankfurt).
byTrain(metz,paris).
byTrain(saarbruecken,paris).

byPlane(frankfurt,bangkok).
byPlane(frankfurt,singapore).
byPlane(paris,losAngeles).
byPlane(bangkok,auckland).
byPlane(singapore,auckland).
byPlane(losAngeles,auckland).
```

Write a predicate travel/2 which determines whether it is possible to travel from one place to another by chaining together car, train, and plane journeys. For example, your program should answer yes to the query travel(valmont,raglan).

3. So, by using travel/2 to query the above database, you can find out that it is possible to go from Valmont to Raglan. If you are planning such a voyage, that's already something useful to know, but you would probably prefer to have the precise route from Valmont to Raglan. Write a predicate travel/3 which tells you which route to take when travelling from one place to another. For example, the program should respond

```
X = go(valmont,metz,
       go(metz,paris,
          go(paris,losAngeles)))
```

to the query travel(valmont,losAngeles,X).

4. Extend the predicate `travel/3` so that it not only tells you the route to take to get from one place to another, but also *how* you have to travel. That is, the new program should let us know, for each stage of the voyage, whether we need to travel by car, train, or plane.

Chapter 4

Lists

This chapter has three main goals:

1. To introduce lists, an important recursive data structure often used in Prolog programming.

2. To define the member/2 predicate, a fundamental Prolog tool for manipulating lists.

3. To introduce the idea of recursing down lists.

1 Lists

As its name suggests, a list is just a plain old list of items. Slightly more precisely, it is a finite sequence of elements. Here are some examples of lists in Prolog:

```
[mia, vincent, jules, yolanda]

[mia, robber(honey_bunny), X, 2, mia]

[]

[mia, [vincent, jules], [butch, girlfriend(butch)]]

[[], dead(z), [2, [b, c]], [], Z, [2, [b, c]]]
```

We can learn some important things from these examples.

elements

length

1. We can specify lists in Prolog by enclosing the elements of the list in square brackets (that is, the symbols [and]). The elements are separated by commas. For example, the first list shown above, [mia, vincent, jules, yolanda], is a list with four elements, namely mia, vincent, jules, and yolanda. The length of a list is the number of elements it has, so our first example is a list of length four.

2. From [mia,robber(honey_bunny),X,2,mia], our second example, we learn that all sorts of Prolog objects can be elements of a list. The first element of this list is mia, an atom; the second element is robber(honey_bunny), a complex term; the third element is X, a variable; the fourth element is 2, a number. Moreover, we also learn that the same item may occur more than once in the same list: for example, the fifth element of this list is mia, which is same as the first element.

empty list

3. The third example shows that there is a special list, the empty list. The empty list (as its name suggests) is the list that contains no elements. What is the length of the empty list? Zero, of course (for the length of a list is the number of members it contains, and the empty list contains nothing).

4. The fourth example teaches us something extremely important: lists can contain other lists as elements. For example, the second element of

[mia, [vincent, jules], [butch,girlfriend(butch)]

is [vincent,jules]. The third is [butch,girlfriend(butch)].

What is the length of the fourth list? The answer is: three. If you thought it was five (or indeed, anything else) you're not thinking about lists in the right way. The elements of the list are the things between the outermost square brackets separated by commas. So this list contains *three* elements: the first element is mia, the second element is [vincent, jules], and the third element is [butch, girlfriend(butch)].

5. The last example mixes all these ideas together. We have here a list which contains the empty list (in fact, it contains it twice), the complex term dead(z), two copies of the list [2, [b, c]], and the variable Z. Note that the third (and the last) elements are lists which themselves contain lists (namely [b, c]).

Now for an important point. Any non-empty list can be thought of as consisting of two parts: the head and the tail. The head is simply the first item in the list; the tail is everything else. To put it more precisely, the tail is the list that remains when we take the first element away; that is, *the tail of a list is always a list*. For example, the head of

[mia, vincent, jules, yolanda]

is mia and the tail is   [vincent, jules, yolanda]. Similarly, the head of

[[], dead(z), [2, [b, c]], [], Z, [2, [b, c]]]

is [], and the tail is [dead(z), [2,[b,c]],[],Z,[2,[b, c]]]. And what are the head and the tail of the list [dead(z)]? Well, the head is the first element of the list, which is dead(z), and the tail is the list that remains if we take the head away, which, in this case, is the empty list [].

What about the empty list? It has neither a head nor a tail. That is, the empty list has no internal structure; for Prolog, [] is a special, particularly simple, list. As we shall learn when we start writing recursive list processing programs, this fact plays an important role in Prolog programming.

Prolog has a special built-in operator | which can be used to decompose a list into its head and tail. It is important to get to know how to use |, for it is a key tool for writing Prolog list manipulation programs.

The most obvious use of | is to extract information from lists. We do this by using | together with unification. For example, to get hold of the head and tail of [mia,vincent, jules,yolanda] we can pose the following query:

```
?- [Head|Tail] = [mia, vincent, jules, yolanda].

Head = mia
Tail = [vincent,jules,yolanda]
yes
```

That is, the head of the list has become bound to Head and the tail of the list has become bound to Tail. Note that there is nothing special about Head and Tail, they are simply variables. We could just as well have posed the query:

```
?- [X|Y] = [mia, vincent, jules, yolanda].

X = mia
Y = [vincent,jules,yolanda]
yes
```

As we mentioned above, only non-empty lists have heads and tails. If we try to use | to pull [] apart, Prolog will fail:

```
?- [X|Y] = [].

    no
```

That is, Prolog treats [] as a special list. This observation is extremely important. We'll see why later.

Let's look at some other examples. We can extract the head and tail of the following list just as we saw above:

```
?- [X|Y] = [[], dead(z), [2, [b, c]], [], Z].

X = []
Y = [dead(z),[2,[b,c]],[],_7800]
Z = _7800
yes
```

That is: the head of the list is bound to X, the tail is bound to Y. (We also learn that Prolog has bound Z to the internal variable _7800.)

But we can do a lot more with |; it really is a flexible tool. For
example, suppose we wanted to know what the first *two* elements of the
list were, and also the remainder of the list after the second element.
Then we'd pose the following query:

```
?- [X,Y | W] = [[], dead(z), [2, [b, c]], [], Z].

X = []
Y = dead(z)
W = [[2,[b,c]],[],_8327]
Z = _8327
yes
```

That is, the head of the list is bound to X, the second element is
bound to Y, and the remainder of the list after the second element is
bound to W (that is, W is the list that remains when we take away the
first two elements). So | can not only be used to split a list into its
head and its tail, we can also use it to split a list at any point. To the
left of | we simply indicate how many elements we want to take away
from the front of the list, and then to right of the | we will get what
remains.

This is a good time to introduce the anonymous variable. Suppose
we were interested in getting hold of the second and fourth elements of
the list:

```
[[], dead(z), [2, [b, c]], [], Z].
```

Now, we could find out like this:

```
?- [X1,X2,X3,X4 | Tail] =
            [[], dead(z), [2, [b, c]], [], Z].

X1 = []
X2 = dead(z)
X3 = [2,[b,c]]
X4 = []
Tail = [_8910]
Z = _8910
yes
```

Ok, we have got the information we wanted: the values we are
interested in are bound to the variables X2 and X4. But we've got a
lot of other information too (namely the values bound to X1, X3 and

Tail). And perhaps we're not interested in all this other stuff. If so, it's a bit silly having to explicitly introduce variables X1, X3 and Tail to deal with it. And in fact, there is a simpler way to obtain *only* the information we want: we can pose the following query instead:

```
?- [_,X,_,Y|_] = [[], dead(z), [2, [b, c]], [], Z].

X = dead(z)
Y = []
Z = _9593
yes
```

The _ symbol (that is, underscore) is the anonymous variable. We use it when we need to use a variable, but we're not interested in what Prolog instantiates the variable to. As you can see in the above example, Prolog didn't bother telling us what _ was bound to. Moreover, note that each occurrence of _ is *independent*: each is bound to something different. This couldn't happen with an ordinary variable of course, but then the anonymous variable isn't meant to be ordinary. It's simply a way of telling Prolog to bind something to a given position, completely independently of any other bindings.

Let's look at one last example. The third element of our working example is a list (namely [2, [b, c]]). Suppose we wanted to extract the tail of this internal list, and that we are not interested in any other information. How could we do this? As follows:

```
?- [_,_,[_|X]|_] =
        [[], dead(z), [2, [b, c]], [], Z, [2, [b, c]]].

X = [[b,c]]
Z = _10087
yes
```

2   Member

It's time to look at our first example of a recursive Prolog program for manipulating lists. One of the most basic things we would like to know is whether something is an element of a list or not. So let's write a program that, when given as inputs an arbitrary object *X* and a list *L*, tells us whether or not *X* belongs to *L*. The program that does this is usually called member, and it is the simplest example of a Prolog program that exploits the recursive structure of lists. Here it is:

member

```
member(X,[X|T]).
member(X,[H|T]) :- member(X,T).
```

That's all there is to it: one fact (namely `member(X,[X|T])`) and one rule (namely `member(X,[H|T]) :- member(X,T)`). But note that the rule is recursive (after all, the functor `member` occurs in both the rule's head and body) and it is this that explains why such a short program is all that is required. Let's take a closer look.

We'll start by reading the program declaratively. And read this way, it is obviously sensible. The first clause (the fact) simply says: an object X is a member of a list if it is the head of that list. Note that we used the built-in | operator to state this (simple but important) principle about lists.

What about the second clause, the recursive rule? This says: an object X is member of a list if it is a member of the tail of the list. Again, note that we used the | operator to state this principle.

Now, clearly this definition makes good declarative sense. But does this program actually *do* what it is supposed to do? That is, will it really tell us whether an object X belongs to a list L? And if so, how exactly does it do this? To answer such questions, we need to think about its procedural meaning. Let's work our way through a few examples.

Suppose we posed the following query:

```
?- member(yolanda,[yolanda,trudy,vincent,jules]).
```

Prolog will immediately answer yes. Why? Because it can unify yolanda with both occurrences of X in the first clause (the fact) in the definition of `member/2`, so it succeeds immediately.

Next consider the following query:

```
?- member(vincent,[yolanda,trudy,vincent,jules]).
```

Now the first rule won't help (vincent and yolanda are distinct atoms) so Prolog goes to the second clause, the recursive rule. This gives Prolog a new goal: it now has to see if

```
member(vincent,[trudy,vincent,jules]).
```

Once again the first clause won't help, so Prolog goes (again) to the recursive rule. This gives it a new goal, namely

```
member(vincent,[vincent,jules]).
```

This time, the first clause does help, and the query succeeds.

So far so good, but we need to ask an important question. What happens when we pose a query that *fails*? For example, what happens if we pose the query

```
member(zed,[yolanda,trudy,vincent,jules]).
```

Now, this should obviously fail (after all, zed is not on the list). So how does Prolog handle this? In particular, how can we be sure that Prolog really will *stop*, and say *no*, instead going into an endless recursive loop?

Let's think this through systematically. Once again, the first clause cannot help, so Prolog uses the recursive rule, which gives it a new goal

```
member(zed,[trudy,vincent,jules]).
```

Again, the first clause doesn't help, so Prolog reuses the recursive rule and tries to show that

```
member(zed,[vincent,jules]).
```

Similarly, the first rule doesn't help, so Prolog reuses the second rule yet again and tries the goal

```
member(zed,[jules]).
```

Again the first clause doesn't help, so Prolog uses the second rule, which gives it the goal

```
member(zed,[])
```

And *this* is where things get interesting. Obviously the first clause can't help here. But note: *the recursive rule can't do anything more either.* Why not? Simple: the recursive rule relies on splitting the list into a head and a tail, but as we have already seen, the empty list *can't* be split up in this way. So the recursive rule cannot be applied either, and Prolog stops searching for more solutions and announces no. That is, it tells us that zed does not belong to the list, which is just what it ought to do.

We could summarise the member/2 predicate as follows. It is a recursive predicate, which systematically searches down the length of the list for the required item. It does this by stepwise breaking down the list into smaller lists, and looking at the first item of each smaller list. This mechanism that drives this search is recursion, and the reason that this recursion is safe (that is, the reason it does not go on forever) is that at the end of the line Prolog has to ask a question about the empty list. The empty list *cannot* be broken down into smaller parts, and this allows a way out of the recursion.

Well, we've now seen why member/2 works, but in fact it's far more useful than the previous example might suggest. Up till now we've only been using it to answer yes/no questions. But we can also pose questions containing variables. For example, we can have the following dialog with Prolog:

```
member(X,[yolanda,trudy,vincent,jules]).

X = yolanda ;

X = trudy ;

X = vincent ;

X = jules ;

no
```

That is, Prolog has told us what every member of a list is. This is an extremely common use of member/2. In effect, by using the variable we are saying to Prolog: "Quick! Give me some element of the list!". In many applications we need to be able to extract members of a list, and this is the way it is typically done.

One final remark. The way we defined member/2 above is certainly correct, but in one respect it is a little messy.

Think about it. The first clause is there to deal with the head of the list. But although the tail is irrelevant to the first clause, we named the tail using the variable T. Similarly, the recursive rule is there to deal with the tail of the list. But although the head is irrelevant here, we named it using the variable H. These unnecessary variable names are distracting: it's better to write predicates in a way that focuses attention on what is really important in each clause, and the anonymous variable gives us a nice way of doing this. That is, we can rewrite member/2 as follows:

```
member(X,[X|_]).
member(X,[_|T]) :- member(X,T).
```

This version is exactly the same, both declaratively and procedurally. But it's just that little bit clearer: when you read it, you are forced to concentrate on what is essential.

3 Recursing down Lists

The member/2 predicate works by recursively working its way down a list, doing something to the head, and then recursively doing the same thing to the tail. Recursing down a list (or indeed, several lists) in this way is extremely common in Prolog; so common, in fact, that it is important that you really master the technique. So let's look at another example.

When working with lists, we often want to compare one list with another, or to copy bits of one list into another, or to translate the contents of one list into another, or something similar. Here's an example. Let's suppose we need a predicate a2b/2 that takes two lists as arguments, and succeeds if the first argument is a list of as, and the second argument is a list of bs of exactly the same length. For example, if we pose the following query

    a2b([a,a,a,a],[b,b,b,b]).

we want Prolog to say yes. On the other hand, if we pose the query

    a2b([a,a,a,a],[b,b,b]).

or the query

    a2b([a,c,a,a],[b,b,5,4]).

we want Prolog to say no.

When faced with such tasks, often the best way to set about solving them is to start by thinking about the simplest possible case. Now, when working with lists, thinking about the simplest case often means thinking about the empty list, and it certainly means this here. After all: what is the shortest possible list of as? It's the empty list. Why? Because it contains no as at all. And what is the shortest possible list of bs? Again, the empty list: no bs whatsoever in that. So the most basic information our definition needs to contain is

    a2b([],[]).

This records the obvious fact that the empty list contains exactly as many as as bs. But although obvious, this fact turns out to play an important role in our program, as we shall see.

So far so good: but how do we proceed? Here's the idea: for longer lists, *think recursively*. So: when should a2b/2 decide that two non-empty lists are a list of as and a list of bs of exactly the same length? Simple: when the head of the first list is an a, and the head of the second list is a b, and a2b/2 decides that the two tails are lists of as and bs of exactly the same length! This immediately gives us the following rule:

```
a2b([a|Ta],[b|Tb]) :- a2b(Ta,Tb).
```

This says: the a2b/2 predicate should succeed if its first argument is a list with head a, its second argument is a list with head b, and a2b/2 succeeds on the two tails.

Now, this definition make good sense declaratively. It is a simple and natural recursive predicate, the base clause dealing with the empty list, the recursive clause dealing with non-empty lists. But how does it work in practice? That is, what is its procedural meaning? For example, if we pose the query

```
a2b([a,a,a],[b,b,b]).
```

Prolog will say yes, which is what we want — but *why* exactly does this happen?

Let's work the example through. In this query, neither list is empty, so the fact does not help. Thus Prolog goes on to try the recursive rule. Now, the query does match the rule (after all, the head of the first list is a and the head of the second is b) so Prolog now has a new goal, namely

```
a2b([a,a],[b,b]).
```

Once again, the fact does not help with this, but the recursive rule can be used again, leading to the following goal:

```
a2b([a],[b]).
```

Yet again the fact does not help, but the recursive rule does, so we get the following goal:

```
a2b([],[]).
```

At last we can use the fact: this tells us that, yes, we really do have two lists here that contain exactly the same number of as and bs (namely, none at all). And because this goal succeeds, this means that the goal

```
a2b([a],[b]).
```

succeeds too. This in turn means that the goal

```
a2b([a,a],[b,b]).
```

succeeds, and thus that the original goal

```
a2b([a,a,a],[b,b,b]).
```

is satisfied.

We could summarise this process as follows. Prolog started with two lists. It peeled the head off each of them, and checked that they were an a and a b, respectively, as required. It then recursively analysed the tails of both lists. That is, it worked its way down both tails simultaneously, checking that at each stage the tails were headed by an a and a b. Why did the process stop? Because at each recursive step we had to work with shorter lists (namely the tails of the lists examined at the previous step) and eventually we ended up with empty lists. At this point, our rather trivial looking fact was able to play a vital role: it said yes. This halted the recursion, and ensured that the original query succeeded.

It's is also important to think about what happens with queries that *fail*. For example, if we pose the query

```
a2b([a,a,a,a],[b,b,b]).
```

Prolog will correctly say no. Why? because after carrying out the peel-off-the-head-and-recursively-examine-the-tail process three times, it will be left with the query

```
a2b([a],[]).
```

But this goal cannot be satisfied. And if we pose the query

```
a2b([a,c,a,a],[b,b,5,4]).
```

after carrying out the peel-off-the-head-and-recursively-examine-the-tail process once, Prolog will have the goal

```
a2b([c,a,a],[b,5,4]).
```

and again, this cannot be satisfied.

Well, that's how a2b/2 works in simple cases, but we haven't exhausted its possibilities yet. As always with Prolog, it's a good idea to investigate what happens when variables as used as input. And with a2b/2 something interesting happens: it acts as a translator, translating lists of as to lists of bs, and vice versa. For example the query

```
a2b([a,a,a,a],X).
```

yields the response

    X = [b,b,b,b].

That is, the list of as has been translated to a list of bs. Similarly, by using a variable in the first argument position, we can use it to translate lists of bs to lists of as:

    a2b(X,[b,b,b,b]).

    X = [a,a,a,a]

And of course, we can use variables in both argument positions:

    a2b(X,Y).

Can you work out what happens in this case?

    To sum up: a2b/2 is an extremely simple example of a program that works by recursing its way down a pair of lists. But don't be fooled by its simplicity: the kind of programming it illustrates is fundamental to Prolog. Both its declarative form (a base clause dealing with the empty list, a recursive clause dealing with non-empty lists) and the procedural idea it trades on (do something to the heads, and then recursively do the same thing to the tails) come up again and again in Prolog programming. In fact, in the course of your Prolog career, you'll find that you'll write what is essentially the a2b/2 predicate, or a more complex variant of it, many times over in many different guises.

4 Exercises

Exercise 4.1. How does Prolog respond to the following queries? $\boxed{\mathcal{E}}$

 1. [a,b,c,d] = [a,[b,c,d]].

 2. [a,b,c,d] = [a|[b,c,d]].

 3. [a,b,c,d] = [a,b,[c,d]].

 4. [a,b,c,d] = [a,b|[c,d]].

 5. [a,b,c,d] = [a,b,c,[d]].

 6. [a,b,c,d] = [a,b,c|[d]].

 7. [a,b,c,d] = [a,b,c,d,[]].

 8. [a,b,c,d] = [a,b,c,d|[]].

9. [] = _.

10. [] = [_].

11. [] = [_|[]].

Exercise 4.2.   Which of the following are syntactically correct lists? If the representation is correct, how many elements does the list have?

1. [1|[2,3,4]]

2. [1,2,3|[]]

3. [1|2,3,4]

4. [1|[2|[3|[4]]]]

5. [1,2,3,4|[]]

6. [[]|[]]

7. [[1,2]|4]

8. [[1,2],[3,4]|[5,6,7]]

Exercise 4.3.   Write a predicate second(X,List) which checks whether X is the second element of List.

Exercise 4.4.   Write a predicate swap12(List1,List2) which checks whether List1 is identical to List2, except that the first two elements are exchanged.

Exercise 4.5.   Suppose we are given a knowledge base with the following facts:

```
tran(eins,one).
tran(zwei,two).
tran(drei,three).
tran(vier,four).
tran(fuenf,five).
tran(sechs,six).
tran(sieben,seven).
tran(acht,eight).
tran(neun,nine).
```

Write a predicate listtran(G,E) which translates a list of German number words to the corresponding list of English number words. For example:

```
listtran([eins,neun,zwei],X).
```

should give:

```
X = [one,nine,two].
```

Your program should also work in the other direction. For example, if you give it the query

```
listtran(X,[one,seven,six,two]).
```

it should return:

```
X = [eins,sieben,sechs,zwei].
```

(Hint: to answer this question, first ask yourself "How do I translate the *empty* list of number words?". That's the base case. For non-empty lists, first translate the head of the list, then use recursion to translate the tail.)

Exercise 4.6.   Write a predicate twice(In,Out) whose left argument is a list, and whose right argument is a list consisting of every element in the left list written twice. For example, the query

```
twice([a,4,buggle],X).
```

should return

```
X = [a,a,4,4,buggle,buggle]).
```

And the query

```
twice([1,2,1,1],X).
```

should return

```
X = [1,1,2,2,1,1,1,1].
```

(Hint: to answer this question, first ask yourself "What should happen when the first argument is the *empty* list?". That's the base case. For non-empty lists, think about what you should do with the head, and use recursion to handle the tail.)

Exercise 4.7.   Draw the search trees for the following three queries:

```
?- member(a,[c,b,a,y]).

?- member(x,[a,b,c]).

?- member(X,[a,b,c]).
```

(Search trees were introduced in Chapter 2.)

5 Practical Session

The purpose of Practical Session 4 is to help you get familiar with the idea of recursing down lists. We first suggest some traces for you to carry out, and then some programming exercises.

First, systematically carry out a number of traces on a2b/2 to make sure you fully understand how it works. In particular:

1. Trace some examples, not involving variables, that succeed. For example, trace the query a2b([a,a,a,a],[b,b,b,b]) and relate the output to the discussion in the text.

2. Trace some simple examples that fail. Try examples involving lists of different lengths (such as a2b([a,a,a,a],[b,b,b])) and examples involving symbols other than a and b (such as a2b([a,c,a,a],[b,b,5,4])).

3. Trace some examples involving variables. For example, try tracing a2b([a,a,a,a],X) and a2b(X,[b,b,b,b]).

4. Make sure you understand what happens when both arguments in the query are variables. For example, carry out a trace on the query a2b(X,Y).

5. Carry out a series of similar traces involving member/2. That is, carry out traces involving simple queries that succeed (such as member(a,[1,2,a,b])), simple queries that fail (such as member(z,[1,2,a,b])), and queries involving variables (such as member(X,[1,2,a,b])). In all cases, make sure that you understand why the recursion halts.

Having done this, try the following.

1. Write a 3-place predicate combine1 which takes three lists as arguments and combines the elements of the first two lists into the third as follows:

    ?- combine1([a,b,c],[1,2,3],X).

    X = [a,1,b,2,c,3]

    ?- combine1([f,b,yip,yup],[glu,gla,gli,glo],Result).

    Result = [f,glu,b,gla,yip,gli,yup,glo]

2. Now write a 3-place predicate `combine2` which takes three lists as arguments and combines the elements of the first two lists into the third as follows:

   ```
   ?- combine2([a,b,c],[1,2,3],X).
   ```

   ```
   X = [[a,1],[b,2],[c,3]]
   ```

   ```
   ?- combine2([f,b,yip,yup],[glu,gla,gli,glo],Result).
   ```

   ```
   Result = [[f,glu],[b,gla],[yip,gli],[yup,glo]]
   ```

3. Finally, write a 3-place predicate `combine3` which takes three lists as arguments and combines the elements of the first two lists into the third as follows:

   ```
   ?- combine3([a,b,c],[1,2,3],X).
   ```

   ```
   X = [j(a,1),j(b,2),j(c,3)]
   ```

   ```
   ?- combine3([f,b,yip,yup],[glu,gla,gli,glo],R).
   ```

   ```
   R = [j(f,glu),j(b,gla),j(yip,gli),j(yup,glo)]
   ```

All three programs are pretty much the same as `a2b/2` (though they manipulate three lists, not two). That is, all three can be written by recursing down the lists, doing something to the heads, and then recursively doing the same thing to the tails. Indeed, once you have written `combine1`, you just need to change what you do to the heads to get `combine2` and `combine3`.

Chapter 5

Arithmetic

This chapter has two main goals:

1. To introduce Prolog's built-in abilities for performing arithmetic.

2. To apply them to simple list processing problems, using accumulators.

1 Arithmetic in Prolog

Prolog provides a number of basic arithmetic tools for manipulating integers (that is, numbers of the form ...-3, -2, -1, 0, 1, 2, 3, 4...). Most Prolog implementation also provide tools for handling real numbers (or floating point numbers) such as 1.53 or 6.35×10^5, but we're not going to discuss these, for they are not particularly useful for the symbolic processing tasks discussed in this book. Integers, on the other hand, are useful in connection with symbolic tasks (we use them to state the length of lists, for example) so it is important to understand how to work with them. We'll start by looking at how Prolog handles the four basic operations of addition, multiplication, subtraction, and division.

Arithmetic examples	Prolog Notation
$6 + 2 = 8$	8 is 6+2.
$6 * 2 = 12$	12 is 6*2.
$6 - 2 = 4$	4 is 6-2.
$6 - 8 = -2$	-2 is 6-8.
$6 \div 2 = 3$	3 is 6/2.
$7 \div 2 = 3$	3 is 7/2.
1 is the remainder when 7 is divided by 2	1 is mod(7,2).

Note that as we are working with integers, division gives us back an integer answer. Thus $7 \div 2$ gives 3 as an answer, leaving remainder 1.

Posing the following queries yields the following responses:

```
?- 8 is 6+2.
yes


?- 12 is 6*2.
yes


?- -2 is 6-8.
yes


?- 3 is 6/2.
yes


?- 1 is mod(7,2).
yes
```

More importantly, we can work out the answers to arithmetic questions by using variables. For example:

```
?- X is 6+2.

X = 8

?- X is 6*2.

X = 12

?- R is mod(7,2).

R = 1
```

Moreover, we can use arithmetic operations when we define predicates. Here's a simple example. Let's define a predicate add_3_and_double/2 whose arguments are both integers. This predicate takes its first argument, adds three to it, doubles the result, and returns the number obtained as the second argument. We define this predicate as follows:

```
add_3_and_double(X,Y) :- Y is (X+3)*2.
```

And indeed, this works:

```
?- add_3_and_double(1,X).

X = 8

?- add_3_and_double(2,X).

X = 10
```

One other thing. Prolog understands the usual conventions we use for disambiguating arithmetical expressions. For example, when we write $3 + 2 \times 4$ we mean $3 + (2 \times 4)$ and not $(3 + 2) \times 4$, and Prolog knows this convention:

```
?- X is 3+2*4.

X = 11
```

2 A Closer Look

That's the basics, but we need to know more. The most important to grasp is this: +, *, -, ÷ and mod do *not* carry out any arithmetic. In fact, expressions such as 3+2, 3-2 and 3*2 are simply terms. The functors of these terms are +, – and * respectively, and the arguments are 3 and 2. Apart from the fact that the functors go between their arguments (instead of in front of them) these are ordinary Prolog terms, and unless we do something special, Prolog will not actually do any arithmetic. In particular, if we pose the query

```
?- X = 3+2
```

we don't get back the answer X=5. Instead we get back

```
X = 3+2
yes
```

That is, Prolog has simply unified the variable X to the complex term 3+2. It has *not* carried out any arithmetic. It has simply done what it usually does when =/2 is used: performed unification.

Similarly, if we pose the query

```
?- 3+2*5 = X
```

we get the response

```
X = 3+2*5
yes
```

Again, Prolog has simply bound the variable X to the complex term 3+2*5. It did not evaluate this expression to 13.

To force Prolog to actually evaluate arithmetic expressions we have to use

```
is
```

just as we did in our earlier examples. In fact, is does something very special: it sends a signal to Prolog that says "Hey! Don't treat this expression as an ordinary complex term! Call up your built-in arithmetic capabilities and carry out the calculations!"

In short, is forces Prolog to act in an unusual way. Normally Prolog is quite happy just unifying variables to structures: that's its job, after all. Arithmetic is something extra that has been bolted on to the basic Prolog engine because it is useful. Unsurprisingly, there are some restrictions on this extra ability, and we need to know what they are.

For a start, the arithmetic expressions to be evaluated must be on the right hand side of is. In our earlier examples we carefully posed the query

```
?- X is 6+2.
```

```
X = 8
```

which is the right way to do it. If instead we had asked

```
6+2 is X.
```

we would have got a message saying `instantiation_error`, or something similar.

Moreover, although we are free to use variables on the right hand side of `is`, when we actually carry out evaluation, the variable must already have been instantiated to a variable-free arithmetic expression. If the variable is uninstantiated, or if it is instantiated to something other than an integer, we will get some sort of `instantiation_error` message. This is because arithmetic isn't performed using Prolog's usual unification and knowledge base search mechanisms: it's done by calling up a special black box which knows about integer arithmetic. If we hand the black box the wrong kind of data, it's going to complain.

Here's an example. Recall our "add 3 and double it" predicate.

```
add_3_and_double(X,Y) :- Y is (X+3)*2.
```

When we described this predicate, we carefully said that it added 3 to its first argument, doubled the result, and returned the answer in its second argument. For example, `add_3_and_double(3,X)` returns X = 12. We didn't say anything about using this predicate in the reverse direction. For example, we might hope that posing the query

```
?- add_3_and_double(X,12).
```

would return the answer X=3. But it doesn't. Instead we get the `instantiation_error` message. Why? Well, when we pose the query this way round, we are asking Prolog to evaluate 12 is (X+3)*2, which it *can't* do as X is not instantiated.

Two final remarks. As we've already mentioned, for Prolog 3 + 2 is just a term. In fact, for Prolog, it really *is* the term *+(3,2)*. The expression 3 + 2 is just a user-friendly notation that's nicer for us to use. This means that, if you want to, you can give Prolog queries like

```
X is +(3,2)
```

and Prolog will correctly reply

```
X = 5
```

Actually, you can even given Prolog the query

```
?- is(X,+(3,2))
```

and Prolog will respond

```
X = 5
```

This is because, for Prolog, the expression X is +(3,2) really is the term is(X,+(3,2)). The expression X is +(3,2) is just user-friendly notation. Underneath, as always, Prolog is just working away with terms.

Summing up, arithmetic in Prolog is easy to use. Pretty much all you have to remember is to use is to force evaluation, that stuff to be evaluated must go to the right of is, and to take care that any variables are correctly instantiated. But there is a deeper point that is worth reflecting on: bolting on the extra capability to do arithmetic in this way has further widened the gap between the procedural and declarative meanings of Prolog programs.

3 Arithmetic and Lists

Probably the most important use of arithmetic in this book is to tell us useful facts about data-structures, such as lists. For example, it can be useful to know how long a list is. We'll give some examples of using lists together with arithmetic capabilities.

How long is a list? Here's a recursive definition.

1. The empty list has length zero.

2. A non-empty list has length 1 + *len*(T), where *len*(T) is the length of its tail.

This definition is practically a Prolog program already. Here's the code we need:

```
len([],0).
len([_|T],N) :- len(T,X), N is X+1.
```

This predicate works in the expected way. For example:

```
?- len([a,b,c,d,e,[a,b],g],X).
```

```
X = 7
```

Now, this is quite a good program: it's easy to understand and efficient. But there is another method of finding the length of a list. We'll now look at this alternative, because it introduces the idea of accumulators. If you're used to other programming languages, you're probably used to the idea of using variables to hold intermediate results. An accumulator is the Prolog analog of this idea.

accumu-
lators

Here's how to use an accumulator to calculate the length of a list. We shall define a predicate accLen3/ which takes the following arguments.

```
accLen(List,Acc,Length)
```

Here List is the list whose length we want to find, and Length is its length (an integer). What about Acc? This is the accumulator we will use to keep track of intermediate values for length (so it will also be an integer). Here's what we do. When we call this predicate, we are going to give Acc an initial value of 0. We then recursively work our way down the list, adding 1 to Acc each time we find a head element, until we reach the empty list. When we reach the empty list, Acc will contain the length of the list. Here's the code:

```
accLen([_|T],A,L) :-  Anew is A+1, accLen(T,Anew,L).
accLen([],A,A).
```

The base case of the definition, unifies the second and third arguments. Why? Because this trivial unification is a nice way of making sure that the result, that is, the length of the list, is returned. When we reach the end of the list, the accumulator (the second variable) contains the length of the list. So we give this value (via unification) to the length variable (the third variable). Here's an example trace. You can clearly see how the length variable gets its value at the bottom of the recursion and passes it upwards as Prolog is coming out of the recursion.

```
?- accLen([a,b,c],0,L).
   Call: (6) accLen([a, b, c], 0, _G449) ?
   Call: (7) _G518 is 0+1 ?
   Exit: (7) 1 is 0+1 ?
   Call: (7) accLen([b, c], 1, _G449) ?
   Call: (8) _G521 is 1+1 ?
   Exit: (8) 2 is 1+1 ?
   Call: (8) accLen([c], 2, _G449) ?
   Call: (9) _G524 is 2+1 ?
   Exit: (9) 3 is 2+1 ?
   Call: (9) accLen([], 3, _G449) ?
```

```
Exit: (9) accLen([], 3, 3) ?
Exit: (8) accLen([c], 2, 3) ?
Exit: (7) accLen([b, c], 1, 3) ?
Exit: (6) accLen([a, b, c], 0, 3) ?
```

As a final step, we'll define a predicate which calls accLen for us, and gives it the initial value of 0:

```
leng(List,Length) :- accLen(List,0,Length).
```

So now we can pose queries like this:

```
?- leng([a,b,c,d,e,[a,b],g],X).
```

Accumulators are extremely common in Prolog programs. (We'll see another accumulator based program in this chapter, and some more in later chapters.) But why is this? In what way is accLen better than len? After all, it looks more difficult. The answer is that accLen is tail recursive while len is not. In tail recursive programs, the result is fully calculated once we reached the bottom of the recursion and just has to be passed up. In recursive programs which are not tail recursive, there are goals at other levels of recursion which have to wait for the answer from a lower level of recursion before they can be evaluated. To understand this, compare the traces for the queries accLen([a,b,c],0,L) (see above) and len([a,b,c],0,L) (given below). In the first case the result is built while going into the recursion — once the bottom is reached at accLen([],3,_G449), the result is there and only has to be passed up. In the second case the result is built while coming out of the recursion; the result of len([b,c], _G481), for instance, is only computed after the recursive call of len has been completed and the result of len([c],_G489) is known. In short, tail recursive programs have less bookkeeping overhead, and this makes them more efficient.

tail
recursive

```
?- len([a,b,c],L).
   Call: (6) len([a, b, c], _G418) ?
   Call: (7) len([b, c], _G481) ?
   Call: (8) len([c], _G486) ?
   Call: (9) len([], _G489) ?
   Exit: (9) len([], 0) ?
   Call: (9) _G486 is 0+1 ?
   Exit: (9) 1 is 0+1 ?
   Exit: (8) len([c], 1) ?
   Call: (8) _G481 is 1+1 ?
   Exit: (8) 2 is 1+1 ?
```

```
Exit: (7) len([b, c], 2) ?
Call: (7) _G418 is 2+1 ?
Exit: (7) 3 is 2+1 ?
Exit: (6) len([a, b, c], 3) ?
```

4   Comparing Integers

Some Prolog arithmetic predicates actually do carry out arithmetic all by themselves (that is, without the assistance of is). These are the operators that compare integers.

Arithmetic examples	Prolog Notation
$x < y$	X < Y.
$x \leq y$	X =< Y.
$x = y$	X =:= Y.
$x \neq y$	X =\= Y.
$x \geq y$	X >= Y
$x > y$	X > Y

These operators have the obvious meaning:

```
?- 2 < 4.
yes

?- 2 =< 4.
yes

?- 4 =< 4.
yes

?- 4=:=4.
yes

?- 4=\=5.
yes

?- 4=\=4.
no

?- 4 >= 4.
yes

?- 4 > 2.
yes
```

   Moreover, they force both their right hand and left hand arguments to
be evaluated:

```
?- 2 < 4+1.
yes
```

```
?- 2+1 < 4.
yes
```

```
?- 2+1 < 3+2.
yes
```

   Note that =:= is different from =, as the following examples show:

```
?- 4=4.
yes
```

```
?- 2+2 =4.
no
```

```
?- 2+2 =:= 4.
yes
```

That is, = tries to unify its arguments; it does *not* force arithmetic
evaluation. That's =:='s job.

   Whenever we use these operators, we have to take care that any
variables are instantiated. For example, all the following queries lead to
instantiation errors.

```
?- X < 3.
```

```
?- 3 < Y.
```

```
?- X =:= X.
```

Moreover, variables have to be instantiated to *integers*. The query

```
?- X = 3, X < 4.
```

succeeds. But the query

```
?- X = b, X < 4.
```

fails.

Ok, let's now look at an example which puts Prolog's abilities to compare numbers to work. We're going to define a predicate which takes a non-empty list of non-negative integers as its first argument, and returns the maximum integer in the list as its last argument. Again, we'll use an accumulator. As we work our way down the list, the accumulator will keep track of the highest integer found so far. If we find a higher value, the accumulator will be updated to this new value. When we call the program, we set the accumulator to an initial value of 0.

Here's the code. Note that there are *two* recursive clauses:

```
accMax([H|T],A,Max) :-
    H > A,
    accMax(T,H,Max).

accMax([H|T],A,Max) :-
    H =< A,
    accMax(T,A,Max).

accMax([],A,A).
```

The first clause tests if the head of the list is larger than the largest value found so far. If it is, we set the accumulator to this new value, and then recursively work through the tail of the list. The second clause applies when the head is less than or equal to the accumulator; in this case we recursively work through the tail of the list using the old accumulator value. Finally, the base clause unifies the second and third arguments; it gives the highest value we found while going through the list to the last argument.

Here's an example query:

```
?- accMax([1,0,5,4],0,Max).
```

Here the first clause of accMax applies, resulting in the following goal:

```
?- accMax([0,5,4],1,Max).
```

Note the value of the accumulator has changed to 1. Now the second clause of accMax applies, as 0 (the next element of the list) is smaller than 1, the value of the accumulator. This process is repeated until we reach the empty list:

```
?- accMax([5,4],1,Max).
```

```
?- accMax([4],5,Max).
```

```
?- accMax([],5,Max).
```

Now the third clause applies, unifying the variable Max with the value
of the accumulator:

```
Max = 5.
yes
```

Again, it's nice to define a predicate which calls this, and initialises
the accumulator. But wait: what should we initialise the accumulator to?
If you say 0, this means you are assuming that all the numbers in the
list are positive. But suppose we give a list of negative integers as
input. Then we would have

```
?- accMax([-11,-2,-7,-4,-12],0,Max).
```

```
Max = 0
yes
```

This is *not* what we want: the biggest number on the list is -2. Our
use of 0 as the initial value of the accumulator has ruined everything,
because it's bigger than any number on the list.

There's an easy way around this: since our input list will always be a
non-empty list of integers, simply initialise the accumulator to the head
of the list. That way we guarantee that the accumulator is initialised to
a number on the list. The following predicate does this for us:

```
max(List,Max) :-
     List = [H|_],
     accMax(List,H,Max).
```

So we can simply say:

```
max([1,2,46,53,0],X).
```

```
X = 53
yes
```

And furthermore we have:

```
max([-11,-2,-7,-4,-12],X).
```

```
X = -2
yes
```

5 Exercises

Exercise 5.1.   How does Prolog respond to the following queries? $\boxed{\mathcal{E}}$

1. X = 3*4.

2. X is 3*4.

3. 4 is X.

4. X = Y.

5. 3 is 1+2.

6. 3 is +(1,2).

7. 3 is X+2.

8. X is 1+2.

9. 1+2 is 1+2.

10. is(X,+(1,2)).

11. 3+2 = +(3,2).

12. *(7,5) = 7*5.

13. *(7,+(3,2)) = 7*(3+2).

14. *(7,(3+2)) = 7*(3+2).

15. 7*3+2 = *(7,+(3,2)).

16. *(7,(3+2)) = 7*(+(3,2)).

Exercise 5.2. $\boxed{\mathcal{E}}$

1. Define a 2-place predicate increment that holds only when its second argument is an integer one larger than its first argument. For example, increment(4,5) should hold, but increment(4,6) should not.

2. Define a 3-place predicate sum that holds only when its third argument is the sum of the first two arguments. For example, sum(4,5,9) should hold, but sum(4,6,12) should not.

$\boxed{\mathcal{E}}$

Exercise 5.3. Write a predicate `addone/2` whose first argument is a list of integers, and whose second argument is the list of integers obtained by adding 1 to each integer in the first list. For example, the query

```
?- addone([1,2,7,2],X).
```

should give

```
X = [2,3,8,3].
```

6 Practical Session

The purpose of Practical Session 5 is to help you get familiar with Prolog's arithmetic capabilities, and to give you some further practice in list manipulation. To this end, we suggest the following programming exercises:

1. In the text we discussed the 3-place predicate `accMax` which returned the maximum of a list of integers. By changing the code slightly, turn this into a 3-place predicate `accMin` which returns the *minimum* of a list of integers.

2. In mathematics, an n-dimensional vector is a list of numbers of length n. For example, `[2,5,12]` is a 3-dimensional vector, and `[45,27,3,-4,6]` is a 5-dimensional vector. One of the basic operations on vectors is *scalar multiplication*. In this operation, every element of a vector is multiplied by some number. For example, if we scalar multiply the 3-dimensional vector `[2,7,4]` by 3 the result is the 3-dimensional vector `[6,21,12]`.

   Write a 3-place predicate `scalarMult` whose first argument is an integer, whose second argument is a list of integers, and whose third argument is the result of scalar multiplying the second argument by the first. For example, the query

   ```
   ?- scalarMult(3,[2,7,4],Result).
   ```

   should yield

   ```
   Result = [6,21,12]
   ```

3. Another fundamental operation on vectors is the *dot product*. This operation combines two vectors of the same dimension and yields a number as a result. The operation is carried out as follows: the corresponding elements of the two vectors are multiplied, and

the results added. For example, the dot product of [2,5,6] and [3,4,1] is 6+20+6, that is, 32. Write a 3-place predicate dot whose first argument is a list of integers, whose second argument is a list of integers of the same length as the first, and whose third argument is the dot product of the first argument with the second. For example, the query

```
?- dot([2,5,6],[3,4,1],Result).
```

should yield

```
Result = 32
```

Chapter 6

More Lists

This chapter has two main goals:

1. To define append/3, a predicate for concatenating two lists, and illustrate what can be done with it.

2. To discuss two ways of reversing a list: a naive method using append/3, and a more efficient method using accumulators.

1 Append

We shall define an important predicate append/3 whose arguments are all lists. Viewed declaratively, append(L1,L2,L3) will hold when the list L3 is the result of concatenating the lists L1 and L2 together (concatenating means joining the lists together, end to end). For example, if we pose the query

```
?- append([a,b,c],[1,2,3],[a,b,c,1,2,3]).
```

concatena-
ting

or the query

```
?- append([a,[foo,gibble],c],[1,2,[[],b]],
          [a,[foo,gibble],c,1,2,[[],b]]).
```

we will get the response yes. On the other hand, if we pose the query

```
?- append([a,b,c],[1,2,3],[a,b,c,1,2]).
```

or the query

```
?- append([a,b,c],[1,2,3],[1,2,3,a,b,c]).
```

we will get the answer no.

From a procedural perspective, the most obvious use of append/3 is to concatenate two lists together. We can do this simply by using a variable as the third argument: the query

```
?- append([a,b,c],[1,2,3],L3).
```

yields the response

```
L3 = [a,b,c,1,2,3]
yes
```

But (as we shall soon see) we can also use append/3 to split up a list. In fact, append/3 is a real workhorse. There's lots we can do with it, and studying it is a good way to gain a better understanding of list processing in Prolog.

Defining append

Here's how append/3 is defined:

```
append([],L,L).
append([H|T],L2,[H|L3]) :- append(T,L2,L3).
```

This is a recursive definition.   The base case simply says that appending the empty list to any list whatsoever yields that same list, which is obviously true.

But what about the recursive step? This says that when we concatenate a non-empty list [H|T] with a list L2, we end up with the list whose head is H and whose tail is the result of concatenating T with L2. It may be useful to think about this definition pictorially:

Input: [H | T] + L2

Result: [H | L3]

T + L2

But what is the procedural meaning of this definition?   What actually goes on when we use append/3 to glue two lists together? Let's take a detailed look at what happens when we pose the query ?- append([a,b,c],[1,2,3],X).

When we pose this query, Prolog will match it to the head of the recursive rule, generating a new internal variable (say _G518) in the process. If we carried out a trace of what happens next, we would get something like the following:

```
append([a, b, c], [1, 2, 3], _G518)
append([b, c], [1, 2, 3], _G587)
append([c], [1, 2, 3], _G590)
append([], [1, 2, 3], _G593)
append([], [1, 2, 3], [1, 2, 3])
append([c], [1, 2, 3], [c, 1, 2, 3])
append([b, c], [1, 2, 3], [b, c, 1, 2, 3])
append([a, b, c], [1, 2, 3], [a, b, c, 1, 2, 3])

X = [a, b, c, 1, 2, 3]
yes
```

The basic pattern should be clear: in the first four lines we see that Prolog recurses its way down the list in its first argument until it can apply the base case of the recursive definition. Then, as the next four lines show, it then stepwise 'fills in' the result. How is this 'filling in' process carried out? By successively instantiating the variables _G593, _G590, _G587, and _G518.   But while it's important to grasp this basic pattern, it doesn't tell us all we need to know about the way append/3 works, so let's dig deeper. Here is the search tree for the query append([a,b,c],[1,2,3],X). We'll work carefully through all the steps, making a careful note of what our goals are, and what the variables are instantiated to.

```
        ┌─────────────────────────────────────────┐
        │ ?- append([a,b,c],[1,2,3],_G518)        │
        └─────────────────────────────────────────┘
_G518 = [a|_G587]                    │
                 ┌────────────────────────────────────────┐
                 │ ?- append([b,c],[1,2,3],_G587)          │
                 └────────────────────────────────────────┘
_G587 = [b|_G590]                         │
_G518 = [a,b|_G590]
                     ┌────────────────────────────────────┐
                     │ ?- append([c],[1,2,3],_G590)        │
                     └────────────────────────────────────┘
_G590 = [c|_G593]                            │
_G587 = [b,c|_G593]
_G518 = [a,b,c|_G593]
                        ┌─────────────────────────────────┐
                        │ ?- append([],[1,2,3],_G593)      │
                        └─────────────────────────────────┘
_G593 = [1,2,3]                                 │
_G590 = [c,1,2,3]
_G587 = [b,c,1,2,3]
_G518 = [a,b,c,1,2,3]                           │
                                                □
```

1. Goal 1: append([a,b,c],[1,2,3],_G518). Prolog matches this to the head of the recursive rule (that is, append([H|T],L2,[H|L3])). Thus _G518 is unified to [a|L3], and Prolog has the new goal append([b,c],[1,2,3],L3). It generates a new variable _G587 for L3, thus we have that _G518 = [a|_G587].

2. Goal 2: append([b,c],[1,2,3],_G587). Prolog matches this to the head of the recursive rule, thus _G587 is unified to [b|L3], and Prolog has the new goal append([c],[1,2,3],L3). It generates the internal variable _G590 for L3, thus we have that _G587 = [b|_G590].

3. Goal 3: append([c],[1,2,3],_G590). Prolog matches this to the head of the recursive rule, thus _G590 is unified to [c|L3], and Prolog has the new goal append([],[1,2,3],L3). It generates the internal variable _G593 for L3, thus we have that _G590 = [c|_G593].

4. Goal 4: append([],[1,2,3],_G593). At last: Prolog can use the base clause (that is, append([],L,L)). And in the four successive matching steps, Prolog will obtain answers to Goal 4, Goal 3, Goal 2, and Goal 1. Here's how.

5. Answer to Goal 4: append([],[1,2,3],[1,2,3]). This is because when we match Goal 4 (that is, append([],[1,2,3],_G593) to the base clause, _G593 is unified to [1,2,3].

6. Answer to Goal 3: append([c],[1,2,3],[c,1,2,3]). Why? Because Goal 3 is append([c],[1,2,3],_G590]), and _G590 is the list [c|_G593], and we have just unified _G593 to [1,2,3]. So _G590 is unified to [c,1,2,3].

7. Answer to Goal 2: append([b,c],[1,2,3],[b,c,1,2,3]). Why? Because Goal 2 is append([b,c],[1,2,3],_G587]), and _G587 is the list [b|_G590], and we have just unified _G590 to [c,1,2,3]. So _G587 is unified to [b,c,1,2,3].

8. Answer to Goal 1: append([a,b,c],[1,2,3],[b,c,1,2,3]). Why? Because Goal 2 is append([a,b,c],[1,2,3],_G518]), and _G518 is the list [a|_G587], and we have just unified _G587 to [b,c,1,2,3]. So _G518 is unified to [a,b,c,1,2,3].

9. Thus Prolog now knows how to instantiate X, the original query variable. It tells us that X = [a,b,c,1,2,3], which is what we want.

Work through this example carefully, and make sure you fully understand the pattern of variable instantiations, namely:

```
_G518 = [a|_G587]
      = [a|[b|_G590]]
      = [a|[b|[c|_G593]]]
```

This type of pattern lies at the heart of the way append/3 works. Moreover, it illustrates a more general theme: the use of unification to build structure. In a nutshell, the recursive calls to append/3 build up this nested pattern of variables which code up the required answer. When

Prolog finally instantiates the innermost variable _G593 to [1, 2, 3], the answer crystallises out, like a snowflake forming around a grain of dust. But it is unification, not magic, that produces the result.

Using append

Now that we understand how append/3 works, let's see how we can put it to work.

One important use of append/3 is to split up a list into two consecutive lists. For example:

```
?- append(X,Y,[a,b,c,d]).

X = []
Y = [a,b,c,d] ;

X = [a]
Y = [b,c,d] ;

X = [a,b]
Y = [c,d] ;

X = [a,b,c]
Y = [d] ;

X = [a,b,c,d]
Y = [] ;

no
```

That is, we give the list we want to split up (here [a,b,c,d]) to append/3 as the third argument, and we use variables for the first two arguments. Prolog then searches for ways of instantiating the variables to two lists that concatenate to give the third argument, thus splitting up the list in two. Moreover, as this example shows, by backtracking, Prolog can find all possible ways of splitting up a list into two consecutive lists.

This ability means it is easy to define some useful predicates with append/3. Let's consider some examples. First, we can define a

prefixes

program which finds prefixes of lists. For example, the prefixes of [a,b,c,d] are [], [a], [a,b], [a,b,c], and [a,b,c,d]. With the help of append/3 it is straightforward to define a program prefix/2, whose arguments are both lists, such that prefix(P,L) will hold when P is a prefix of L. Here's how:

```
prefix(P,L):- append(P,_,L).
```

This says that list P is a prefix of list L when there is some list such that L is the result of concatenating P with that list. (We use the anonymous variable since we don't care what that other list is: we only care that there is some such list or other.) This predicate successfully finds prefixes of lists, and moreover, via backtracking, finds them all:

```
?- prefix(X,[a,b,c,d]).

X = [] ;

X = [a] ;

X = [a,b] ;

X = [a,b,c] ;

X = [a,b,c,d] ;

no
```

In a similar fashion, we can define a program which finds suffixes of lists. For example, the suffixes of [a,b,c,d] are [], [d], [c,d], [b,c,d], and [a,b,c,d]. Again, using append/3 it is easy to define suffix/2, a predicate whose arguments are both lists, such that suffix(S,L) will hold when S is a suffix of L:

```
suffix(S,L):- append(_,S,L).
```

That is, list S is a suffix of list L if there is some list such that L is the result of concatenating that list with S. This predicate successfully finds suffixes of lists, and moreover, via backtracking, finds them all:

```
?- suffix(X,[a,b,c,d]).

X = [a,b,c,d] ;

X = [b,c,d] ;

X = [c,d] ;

X = [d] ;
```

```
X = [] ;
```

no

Make sure you understand why the results come out in this order.

sublists   And now it's very easy to define a program that finds sublists of lists. The sublists of [a,b,c,d] are [], [a], [b], [c], [d], [a,b], [b,c], [c,d], [a,b,c], [b,c,d], and [a,b,c,d]. A little thought reveals that the sublists of a list L are simply the *prefixes of suffixes of* L. Think about it pictorially:

Take suffix: $\boxed{a, b, c, d, e, f, g, \underbrace{h, i, j, k, l}, m, n, o, p}$

Take prefix: $\boxed{\underbrace{h, i, j, k, l}, m, n, o, p}$

Result: $\boxed{h, i, j, k, l}$

As we already have defined the predicates for producing suffixes and prefixes of lists, we simply define a sublist as:

```
sublist(SubL,L):- suffix(S,L), prefix(SubL,S).
```

That is, SubL is a sublist of L if there is some suffix S of L of which SubL is a prefix. This program doesn't *explicitly* use append/3, but of course, under the surface, that's what's doing the work for us, as both prefix/2 and suffix/2 are defined using append/3.

2 Reversing a List

The append/3 predicate is useful, and it is important to know how to put it to work. But it is just as important to know that it can be a source of inefficiency, and that you probably don't want to use it all the time.

Why is append/3 a source of inefficiency? If you think about the way it works, you'll notice a weakness: append/3 doesn't join two lists in one simple action. Rather, it needs to work its way down its first argument until it finds the end of the list, and only then can it carry out the concatenation.

Now, often this causes no problems. For example, if we have two lists and we just want to concatenate them, it's probably not too bad. Sure, Prolog will need to work down the length of the first list, but if the list is not too long, that's probably not too high a price to pay for the ease of working with append/3.

But matters may be very different if the first two arguments are given as variables. As we've just seen, it can be very useful to give append/3 variables in its first two arguments, for this lets Prolog search for ways of splitting up the lists. But there is a price to pay: a lot of searching is going on, and this can lead to very inefficient programs.

To illustrate this, we shall examine the problem of reversing a list. That is, we will examine the problem of defining a predicate which takes a list (say [a,b,c,d]) as input and returns a list containing the same elements in the reverse order (here [d,c,b,a]).

Now, a reverse predicate is a useful predicate to have around. As you will have realised by now, lists in Prolog are far easier to access from the front than from the back. For example, to pull out the head of a list L, all we have to do is perform the unification [H|_] = L; this results in H being instantiated to the head of L. But pulling out the last element of an arbitrary list is harder: we can't do it simply using unification. On the other hand, if we had a predicate which reversed lists, we could first reverse the input list, and then pull out the head of the reversed list, as this would give us the last element of the original list. So a reverse predicate could be a useful tool. However, as we may have to reverse large lists, we would like this tool to be efficient. So we need to think about the problem carefully.

And that's what we're going to do now. We will define two reverse predicates: a naive one, defined with the help of append/3, and a more efficient (and indeed, more natural) one defined using accumulators.

Naive reverse using append

Here's a recursive definition of what is involved in reversing a list:

1. If we reverse the empty list, we obtain the empty list.

2. If we reverse the list [H|T], we end up with the list obtained by reversing T and concatenating with [H].

To see that the recursive clause is correct, consider the list [a,b,c,d]. If we reverse the tail of this list we obtain [d,c,b]. Concatenating this with [a] yields [d,c,b,a], which is the reverse of [a,b,c,d].

With the help of append/3 it is easy to turn this recursive definition into Prolog:

```
naiverev([],[]).
naiverev([H|T],R):- naiverev(T,RevT), append(RevT,[H],R).
```

Now, this definition is correct, but it does an awful lot of work. It is *very* instructive to look at a trace of this program. This shows that the program is spending a lot of time carrying out appends. This shouldn't be too surprising: after, all, we are calling append/3 recursively. The result is very inefficient (if you run a trace, you will find that it takes about 90 steps to reverse an eight element list) and hard to understand (the predicate spends most of its time in the recursive calls to append/3, making it very hard to see what is going on).

Not nice. But as we shall now see, there *is* a better way.

Reverse using an accumulator

The better way is to use an accumulator. The underlying idea is simple and natural. Our accumulator will be a list, and when we start it will be empty. Suppose we want to reverse [a,b,c,d]. At the start, our accumulator will be []. So we simply take the head of the list we are trying to reverse and add it as the head of the accumulator. We then carry on processing the tail, thus we are faced with the task of reversing [b,c,d], and our accumulator is [a]. Again we take the head of the list we are trying to reverse and add it as the head of the accumulator (thus our new accumulator is [b,a]) and carry on trying to reverse [c,d]. Again we use the same idea, so we get a new accumulator [c,b,a], and try to reverse [d]. Needless to say, the next step yields an accumulator [d,c,b,a] and the new goal of trying to reverse []. This is where the process stops: *and our accumulator contains the reversed list we want.* To summarise: the idea is simply to work our way through the list we want to reverse, and push each element in turn onto the head of the accumulator, like this:

```
List: [a,b,c,d]  Accumulator: []
List: [b,c,d]    Accumulator: [a]
List: [c,d]      Accumulator: [b,a]
List: [d]        Accumulator: [c,b,a]
List: []         Accumulator: [d,c,b,a]
```

This will be efficient because we simply blast our way through the list once: we don't have to waste time carrying out concatenation or other irrelevant work.

It's also easy to put this idea in Prolog. Here's the accumulator code:

```
accRev([H|T],A,R):- accRev(T,[H|A],R).
accRev([],A,A).
```

This is classic accumulator code: it follows the same pattern as the arithmetic examples we examined in the previous chapter. The recursive clause is responsible for chopping off the head of the input list, and pushing it onto the accumulator. The base case halts the program, and copies the accumulator to the final argument.

As is usual with accumulator code, it's a good idea to write a predicate which carries out the required initialisation of the accumulator for us:

```
rev(L,R):- accRev(L,[],R).
```

Again, it is instructive to run some traces on this program and compare it with `naiverev/2`. The accumulator based version is *clearly* better. For example, it takes about 20 steps to reverse an eight element list, as opposed to 90 for the naive version. Moreover, the trace is far easier to follow. The idea underlying the accumulator based version is simpler and more natural than the recursive calls to `append/3`.

Summing up, `append/3` is a useful program, and you certainly should not be scared of using it. However, you also need to be aware that it is a source of inefficiency, so when you use it, ask yourself whether there is a better way. And often there is. The use of accumulators is often better, and (as the `reverse/2` example show) accumulators can be a natural way of handling list processing tasks.

3 Exercises

Exercise 6.1.   Let's call a list *doubled* if it is made of two consecutive blocks of elements that are exactly the same. For example, [a,b,c,a,b,c] is doubled (it's made up of [a,b,c] followed by [a,b,c]) and so is [foo,gubble,foo,gubble]. On the other hand, [foo,gubble,foo] is not doubled. Write a predicate doubled(List) which succeeds when List is a doubled list.

Exercise 6.2.   A palindrome is a word or phrase that spells the same forwards and backwards. For example, 'rotator', 'eve', and 'nurses run' are all palindromes. Write a predicate palindrome(List), which checks whether List is a palindrome. For example, to the queries

```
?- palindrome([r,o,t,a,t,o,r]).
```

and

```
?- palindrome([n,u,r,s,e,s,r,u,n]).
```

Prolog should respond yes, but to the query

```
?- palindrome([n,o,t,h,i,s]).
```

it should respond no.

Exercise 6.3.   Write a predicate `toptail(InList,OutList)` which says no if `InList` is a list containing fewer than 2 elements, and which deletes the first and the last elements of `InList` and returns the result as `OutList`, when `InList` is a list containing at least 2 elements. For example:

```
toptail([a],T).
no

toptail([a,b],T).
T=[]

toptail([a,b,c],T).
T=[b]
```

(Hint: here's where `append/3` comes in useful.)

Exercise 6.4.   Write a predicate `last(List,X)` which is true only when `List` is a list that contains at least one element and `X` is the last element of that list. Do this in two different ways:

1. Define `last/2` using the predicate `reverse/2` discussed in the text.

2. Define `last/2` using recursion.

Exercise 6.5.   Write a predicate `swapfl(List1,List2)` which checks whether `List1` is identical to `List2`, except that the first and last elements are exchanged. Here's where `append/3` could come in useful again, but it is also possible to write a recursive definition without appealing to `append/3` (or any other) predicates.

Exercise 6.6.   Here is an exercise for those of you who like logic puzzles.

There is a street with three neighbouring houses that all have a different colour, namely red, blue, and green. People of different nationalities live in the different houses and they all have a different pet. Here are some more facts about them:

- The Englishman lives in the red house.

- The jaguar is the pet of the Spanish family.

- The Japanese lives to the right of the snail keeper.

- The snail keeper lives to the left of the blue house.

Who keeps the zebra? Don't work it out for yourself: define a predicate zebra/1 that tells you the nationality of the owner of the zebra!

(Hint: Think of a representation for the houses and the street. Code the four constraints in Prolog. You may find member/2 and sublist/2 useful.)

4 Practical Session

The purpose of Practical Session 6 is to help you get more experience with list manipulation. We first suggest some traces for you to carry out, and then some programming exercises.

The following traces will help you get to grips with the predicates discussed in the text:

1. Carry out traces of append/3 with the first two arguments instantiated, and the third argument uninstantiated. For example, append([a,b,c],[[],[2,3],b],X) Make sure the basic pattern is clear.

2. Next, carry out traces on append/3 as used to split up a list, that is, with the first two arguments given as variables, and the last argument instantiated. For example, append(L,R,[foo,wee,blup]).

3. Carry out some traces on prefix/2 and suffix/2. Why does prefix/2 find shorter lists first, and suffix/2 longer lists first?

4. Carry out some traces on sublist/2. As we said in the text, via backtracking this predicate generates all possible sublists, but as you'll see, it generates several sublists more than once. Do you understand why?

5. Carry out traces on both naiverev/2 and rev/2, and compare their behaviour.

Now for some programming work:

1. It is possible to write a one line definition of the member predicate by making use of append/3. Do so. How does this new version of member compare in efficiency with the standard one?

2. Write a predicate set(InList,OutList) which takes as input an arbitrary list, and returns a list in which each element of the input list appears only once. For example, the query

```
set([2,2,foo,1,foo, [],[]],X).
```

should yield the result

```
X = [2,foo,1,[]].
```

(Hint: use the `member` predicate to test for repetitions of items you have already found.)

3. We 'flatten' a list by removing all the square brackets around any lists it contains as elements, and around any lists that its elements contain as elements, and so on, for all nested lists. For example, when we flatten the list

```
[a,b,[c,d],[[1,2]],foo]
```

we get the list

```
[a,b,c,d,1,2,foo]
```

and when we flatten the list

```
[a,b,[[[[[[c,d]]]]]],[[1,2]],foo,[]]
```

we also get

```
[a,b,c,d,1,2,foo].
```

Write a predicate `flatten(List,Flat)` that holds when the first argument `List` flattens to the second argument `Flat`. This should be done without making use of `append/3`.

Ok, we're now halfway through the book. And flattening a list is the Pons Asinorum of Prolog programming. Did you cross it ok? If so, great. Time to move on.

Chapter 7

Definite Clause Grammars

This chapter has two main goals:

1. To introduce context free grammars (CFGs) and some related concepts.

2. To introduce definite clause grammars (DCGs), a built-in Prolog mechanism for working with context free grammars (and other kinds of grammar too).

1 Context Free Grammars

Prolog has been used for many purposes, but its inventor, Alain Colmerauer, was interested in computational linguistics, and this remains a classic application for the language. Moreover, Prolog offers a number of tools which make life easier for computational linguists, and we are now going to start learning about one of the most useful of these: definite clause grammars, or DCGs as they are usually called.

definite clause grammars

DCGs are a special notation for defining grammars. So, before we go any further, we'd better learn what a grammar is. We shall do so by discussing context free grammars (or CFGs). The basic idea of context free grammars is simple to understand, but don't be fooled into thinking that CFGs are toys. They're not. While CFGs aren't powerful enough to cope with the syntactic structure of all natural languages (that is, the kind of languages that human beings use), they can certainly handle most aspects of the syntax of many natural languages (for example, English and French) in a reasonably natural way.

grammars

context free grammars

So what is a context free grammar? In essence, a finite collection of rules which tell us that certain sentences are grammatical (that is, syntactically correct) and what their grammatical structure actually is. Here's a simple context free grammar for a small fragment of English:

```
s  -> np vp
np -> det n
vp -> v np
vp -> v
det -> a
det -> the
n  -> woman
n  -> man
v  -> shoots
```

What are the ingredients of this little grammar? Well, first note that it contains three types of symbol. There's ->, which is used to define the rules. Then there are the symbols written like this: s, np, vp, det, n, v. These symbols are called non-terminal symbols; we'll soon learn why. Each of these symbols has a traditional meaning in linguistics: s is short for sentence, np is short for noun phrase, vp is short for verb phrase, and det is short for determiner. That is, each of these symbols is shorthand for a grammatical category. Finally there are the symbols in italics: *a, the, woman, man,* and *shoots.* These are terminal symbols, though a computer scientist might call them the alphabet, and linguists might call them the lexical items. We'll usually just call them words.

non-terminal symbols

terminal symbols

This grammar contains nine context free rules. A context free rule consists of a single non-terminal symbol, followed by ->, followed by a finite sequence made up of terminal and/or non-terminal symbols. All nine items listed above have this form, so they are all legitimate context free rules. What do these rules mean? They tell us how different grammatical categories can be built up. Read -> as *can consist of*, or *can be built out of*. For example, the first rule tells us that a sentence can consist of a noun phrase followed by a verb phrase. The third rule tells us that a verb phrase can consist of a verb followed by a noun phrase, while the fourth rule tells us that there is another way to build a verb phrase: simply use a verb. The last five rules tell us that *a* and *the* are determiners, that *man* and *woman* are nouns, and that *shoots* is a verb.

context free rules

Now consider the string of words *a woman shoots a man*. Is this grammatical according to our little grammar? And if it is, what structure does it have? The following tree answers both questions:

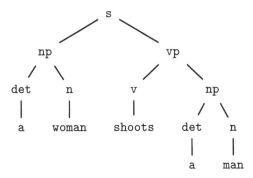

Right at the top we have a node marked s. This node has two daughters, one marked np, and one marked vp. Note that this part of the diagram agrees with the first rule of the grammar, which says that an s can be built out of an np and a vp. (A linguist would say that this part of the tree is licensed by the first rule.) In fact, as you can see, *every* part of the tree is licensed by one of our rules. For example, the two nodes marked np are licensed by the rule that says that an np can consist of a det followed by an n. And, right at the bottom of the diagram, all the words in *a woman shoots a man* are licensed by a rule. Incidentally, note that the terminal symbols only decorate the nodes right at the bottom of the tree (the terminal nodes) while non-terminal symbols only decorate nodes that are higher up in the tree (the non-terminal nodes).

licensed

Such a tree is called a parse tree. Parse trees are important because they give us two kinds of information. Firstly, they give us information about strings. Secondly, they give us information about structure. This is an important distinction to grasp, so let's have a closer look, and learn some important terminology while we are doing so.

First, if we are given a string of words, and a grammar, and it turns out that we *can* build a parse tree like the one above (that is, a tree that has s at the top node, and every node in the tree is licensed by the grammar, and the string of words we were given is listed in the correct order along the terminal nodes) then we say that the string is grammatical (according to the given grammar). For example, the string *a woman shoots a man* is grammatical according to our little grammar (and indeed, any reasonable grammar of English would classify it as grammatical). On the other hand, if there isn't any such tree, the string is ungrammatical (according to the given grammar). For example, the string *woman a woman man a shoots* is ungrammatical according to our little grammar (and any reasonable grammar of English would classify it as ungrammatical). The language generated by a grammar consists of all the strings that the grammar classifies as grammatical. For example, *a woman shoots a man* also belongs to the language generated by our little grammar, and so does *a man shoots the woman*. A context free recogniser is a program which correctly tells us whether or not a string belongs to the language generated by a context free grammar. To put it another way, a recogniser is a program that correctly classifies strings as grammatical or ungrammatical (relative to some grammar).

But often, in both linguistics and computer science, we are not merely interested in whether a string is grammatical or not, we also want to know *why* it is grammatical. More precisely, we often want to know what its structure is, and this is exactly the information a parse tree gives us. For example, the above parse tree shows us how the words in *a woman shoots a man* fit together, piece by piece, to form the sentence. This kind of information would be important if we were using this sentence in some application and needed to say what it actually meant (that is, if we wanted to do semantics). A context free parser is a program which correctly decides whether a string belongs to the language generated by a context free grammar *and also tells us what its structure is*. That is, whereas a recogniser merely says "Yes, grammatical" or "No, ungrammatical" to each string, a parser actually builds the associated parse tree and gives it to us.

Margin terms: parse tree · strings · structure · grammatical · language generated by a grammar · recogniser · parser

It remains to explain one final concept, namely what a context free language is. (Don't get confused: we've told you what a context free *grammar* is, but not what a context free *language* is.) Quite simply, a context free language is a language that can be generated by a context free grammar. Some languages are context free, and some are not. For example, it seems plausible that English is a context free language. That is, it is probably possible to write a context free grammar that generates all (and only) the sentences that native speakers find acceptable. On the other hand, some dialects of Swiss-German are *not* context free. It can be proved mathematically that no context free grammar can generate all (and only) the sentences that native speakers of Swiss-German find acceptable.[1] So if you wanted to write a grammar for such dialects, you would have to employ additional grammatical mechanisms, not merely context free rules.

context
free
language

CFG recognition using append

That's the theory, but how do we work with context free grammars in Prolog? To make things concrete: suppose we are given a context free grammar. How can we write a recogniser for it? And how can we write a parser for it? In this chapter we'll look at the first question in detail. We'll first show how (rather naive) recognisers can be written in Prolog, and then show how more sophisticated recognisers can be written with the help of difference lists. This discussion will lead us to definite clause grammars, Prolog's built-in grammar tool. In the following chapter we'll look at definite clause grammars in more detail, and learn (among other things) how to use them to define parsers.

So: given a context free grammar, how do we define a recogniser in Prolog? In fact, Prolog offers a very direct answer to this question: we can simply write down Prolog clauses that correspond, in an obvious way, to the grammar rules. That is, we can simply turn the grammar into Prolog.

Here's a simple (though as we shall learn, inefficient) way of doing this. We shall use lists to represent strings. For example, we shall use the list [a,woman,shoots,a,man] to represent the string *a woman shoots a man*. Now, we have already said that the -> symbol used in context free grammars means *can consist of*, or *can be built out of*, and this idea is easily modelled using lists. For example, the rule s -> np vp can be thought of as saying: a list of words is an s list if it is the result of concatenating an np list with a vp list. As we know

---

[1]"Evidence against the context-freeness of natural language", Stuart M. Shieber, *Linguistics and Philosophy*, 8:333–343, 1985.

how to concatenate lists in Prolog (we can use append/3), it should be easy to turn these kinds of rules into Prolog. And what about the rules that tell us about individual words? Even easier: we can simply view n -> *woman* as saying that the list [woman] is an n list.

If we turn these ideas into Prolog, this is what we get:

```
s(Z):- np(X), vp(Y), append(X,Y,Z).

np(Z):- det(X), n(Y), append(X,Y,Z).

vp(Z):- v(X), np(Y), append(X,Y,Z).

vp(Z):- v(Z).

det([the]).
det([a]).

n([woman]).
n([man]).

v([shoots]).
```

The correspondence between the CFG rules and the Prolog code should be clear. And to use this program as a recogniser, we simply pose the obvious queries. For example:

```
?- s([a,woman,shoots,a,man]).
yes
```

generate

In fact, because this is a simple declarative Prolog program, we can do more than this: we can also generate all the sentences this grammar produces. Our little grammar generates 20 sentences. Here are the first five:

```
?- s(X).

X = [the,woman,shoots,the,woman] ;

X = [the,woman,shoots,the,man] ;

X = [the,woman,shoots,a,woman] ;

X = [the,woman,shoots,a,man] ;
```

```
X = [the,woman,shoots]
```

Moreover, we're not restricted to posing questions about sentences: we can ask about other grammatical categories. For example:

```
?- np([a,woman]).
yes
```

And we can generate noun phrases with the following query.

```
?- np(X).
```

Now this is rather nice. We have a simple, easy to understand program which corresponds with our CFG in an obvious way. Moreover, if we added more rules to our CFG, it would be easy to alter the program to cope with the new rules.

But there is a problem: the program doesn't use the input sentence to guide the search. Make a trace for the query s([a,man,shoots]) and you will see that the program chooses noun phrases and verb phrases and only afterwards checks whether these can be combined to form the sentence [a,man,shoots]. For example, Prolog will find that [the,woman] is a noun phrase and [shoots,the,woman] a verb phrase and only then will it check whether concatenating these lists happens to yield [a,man,shoots], which of course it won't. So, Prolog starts to backtrack, and the next thing it will try is whether concatenating the noun phrase [the,woman] and the verb phrase [shoots,the,man] happens to yield [a,man,shoots], another non-starter. It will go on like this until it (finally) produces the noun phrase [a,man] and the verb phrase [shoots]. The problem is that the goals np(X) and vp(Y) are called with uninstantiated variables as arguments.

So, how about changing the rules in such a way that append becomes the first goal:

```
s(Z):- append(X,Y,Z), np(X), vp(Y).

np(Z):- append(X,Y,Z), det(X), n(Y).

vp(Z):-  append(X,Y,Z), v(X), np(Y).

vp(Z):-  v(Z).

det([the]).
det([a]).
```

```
n([woman]).
n([man]).

v([shoots]).
```

Here we first use `append/3` to split up the input list. This instantiates the variables X and Y, so that the other goals are all called with instantiated arguments. However, this program is still not very appealing: it uses `append/3` a lot and, even worse, it uses `append/3` with uninstantiated variables in the first two arguments. We saw in the previous chapter that this is a source of inefficiency. And indeed, the performance of this recogniser is very bad. It is revealing to trace through what actually happens when this program analyses a sentence such as *a woman shoots a man*. As you will see, relatively few of the steps are devoted to the real task of recognising the sentences: most are devoted to using `append/3` to decompose lists. This isn't much of a problem for our little grammar, but it certainly would be if we were working with a more realistic grammar capable of generating a large number of sentences. We need to do something about this.

CFG recognition using difference lists

A more efficient implementation can be obtained by making use of *difference lists*. This is a sophisticated (and, once you've grasped it, beautiful) Prolog technique that can be used for a variety of purposes.

The key idea underlying difference lists is to represent the information about grammatical categories not as a single list, but as the difference between two lists. For example, instead of representing *a woman shoots a man* as `[a,woman,shoots,a,man]` we can represent it as the pair of lists

`[a,woman,shoots,a,man] []`.

Think of the first list as *what needs to be consumed* (or if you prefer: the *input list*), and the second list as *what we should leave behind* (or: the *output list*). Viewed from this (rather procedural) perspective the difference list

`[a,woman,shoots,a,man] []`.

represents the sentence *a woman shoots a man* because it says: *If I consume all the symbols on the left, and leave behind the symbols on the right, then I have the sentence I am interested in.* That is, the sentence we are interested in is the difference between the contents of these two lists.

That's all we need to know about difference lists to rewrite our recogniser. If we simply bear in mind the idea of consuming something, and leaving something behind in mind, we obtain the following recogniser:

```
s(X,Z):- np(X,Y), vp(Y,Z).

np(X,Z):- det(X,Y), n(Y,Z).

vp(X,Z):- v(X,Y), np(Y,Z).

vp(X,Z):- v(X,Z).

det([the|W],W).
det([a|W],W).

n([woman|W],W).
n([man|W],W).

v([shoots|W],W).
```

Consider these rules carefully. For example, the s rule says: *I know that the pair of lists* X *and* Z *represents a sentence if (1) I can consume* X *and leave behind a* Y, *and the pair* X *and* Y *represents a noun phrase, and (2) I can then go on to consume* Y *leaving* Z *behind, and the pair* Y Z *represents a verb phrase.* The np rule and the second of the vp rules work similarly.

Moreover, the same idea underlies the way this grammar handles the words. For example

```
n([man|W],W).
```

means we are handling *man* as the difference between [man|W] and W. After all, the difference between what is consumed and what is left behind is precisely the word man.

Now, at first this code may be harder to grasp than our previous recogniser. But note that we have gained something important: *we haven't used* append/3. In the difference list based recogniser, it simply isn't needed, and this makes a big difference.

How do we use this recogniser? Well, here's how to recognise sentences:

```
?- s([a,woman,shoots,a,man],[]).
yes
```

This asks whether we can get an s by consuming the symbols in [a,woman,shoots,a,man], leaving nothing behind. Similarly, to generate all the sentences in the grammar, we ask

```
?- s(X,[]).
```

This asks: what values can you give to X, such that we get an s by consuming the symbols in X, leaving nothing behind?

The queries for other grammatical categories also work the same way. For example, to find out if *a woman* is a noun phrase we ask:

```
?- np([a,woman],[]).
```

And we generate all the noun phrases in the grammar as follows:

```
?- np(X,[]).
```

You should trace what happens when this program analyses a sentence such as *a woman shoots a man*. As you will see, it is a lot more efficient than our append/3 based program. Moreover, as no use is made of append/3, the trace is a lot easier to grasp. So we have taken a big step forward.

On the other hand, it has to be admitted that the second recogniser is not as easy to understand, at least at first, and it's a pain having to keep track of all those difference list variables. If only it were possible to have a recogniser as simple as the first and as efficient as the second. And in fact, it *is* possible: this is where DCGs come in.

2   Definite Clause Grammars

So, what are DCGs? Quite simply, a nice notation for writing grammars that hides the underlying difference list variables. Let's look at three examples.

A first example

As our first example, here's our little grammar written as a DCG:

```
s --> np,vp.

np --> det,n.

vp --> v,np.
```

```
vp --> v.

det --> [the].
det --> [a].

n --> [woman].
n --> [man].

v --> [shoots].
```

The link with the original context free grammar should be transparent: this is definitely the most user-friendly notation we have used yet. But how do we use this DCG? In fact, we use it in *exactly* the same way as we used our difference list recogniser. For example, to find out whether *a woman shoots a man* is a sentence, we pose the query:

```
?- s([a,woman,shoots,a,man],[]).
```

That is, just as in the difference list recogniser, we ask whether we can get an s by consuming the symbols in [a,woman,shoots,a,man], leaving nothing behind.

Similarly, to generate all the sentences in the grammar, we pose the query:

```
?- s(X,[]).
```

This asks what values we can give to X, such that we get an s by consuming the symbols in X, leaving nothing behind.

Moreover, the queries for other grammatical categories also work the same way. For example, to find out if *a woman* is a noun phrase we pose the query:

```
?- np([a,woman],[]).
```

And we generate all the noun phrases in the grammar as follows:

```
?- np(X,[]).
```

What's going on? Quite simply, this DCG *is* our difference list recogniser! To put it another way, DCG notation is essentially syntactic sugar, user-friendly notation that lets us write grammars in a natural way. But Prolog translates this notation into the kinds of difference lists discussed before. So we have the best of both worlds: a nice simple notation for working with, and the efficiency of difference lists.

There is an easy way to see what Prolog translates DCG rules into. Suppose you are working with the DCG just given (that is, suppose that Prolog has already consulted the rules). Then if you pose the query:

```
?- listing(s).
```

you will get the response

```
s(A,B) :-
    np(A,C),
    vp(C,B).
```

This is what Prolog has translated s --> np,vp into. Note that (apart from the choice of variables) this is exactly the difference list rule we used in our second recogniser.

Similarly, if you pose the query

```
?- listing(np).
```

you will get

```
np(A,B) :-
    det(A,C),
    n(C,B).
```

This is what Prolog has translated np --> det,n into. Again (apart from the choice of variables) this is the difference list rule we used in our second recogniser.

To get a complete listing of the translations of all the rules, simply type

```
?- listing.
```

There is one thing you may observe. Some Prolog implementations translate rules such as

```
det --> [the].
```

not into

```
det([the|W],W).
```

which was the form we used in our difference list recogniser, but into

```
det(A,B) :-
    'C'(A,the,B).
```

But although the notation is different, the idea is the same. This says you can get a list B from a list A by consuming a the. That is, once again this is a difference list representation. Note that 'C' is an atom.

Adding recursive rules

Our original context free grammar generated only 20 sentences. However it is easy to write context free grammars that generate infinitely many sentences: simply use recursive rules. Here's an example. Let's add the following rules to our little grammar:

$$s \to s \; conj \; s$$
$$conj \to and$$
$$conj \to or$$
$$conj \to but$$

This rule allows us to join as many sentences together as we like using the words *and*, *but*, and *or*. So this grammar classifies sentences such as *The woman shoots the man or the man shoots the woman* as grammatical.

Now, in principle it is easy to turn this grammar into a DCG. We need merely add the rules

```
s --> s,conj,s.

conj --> [and].
conj --> [or].
conj --> [but].
```

But there is a problem lurking under the surface. What does Prolog actually *do* with this DCG? Let's have a look.

First, let's add the new rules at the *beginning* of the knowledge base, before the rule s --> np,vp. What happens if we then pose the query s([a,woman,shoots],[])? Prolog immediately goes into a loop.

Can you see why? The point is this. Prolog translates DCG rules into ordinary Prolog rules. If we place the recursive rule s --> s,conj,s in the knowledge base before the non-recursive rule s --> np,vp then the knowledge base will contain the following two Prolog rules, in this order:

```
s(A, B) :-
        s(A, C),
        conj(C, D),
        s(D, B).

s(A, B) :-
        np(A, C),
        vp(C, B).
```

Now, from a declarative perspective this is fine, but from a procedural perspective this is fatal. When it tries to use the first rule, Prolog immediately encounters the goal s(A,C), which it then tries to satisfy using the first rule, whereupon it immediately encounters the goal s(A, C), which it then tries to satisfy using the first rule, whereupon it immediately encounters the goal s(A, C), and so on. In short, it goes into an infinite loop and does no useful work.

So let's add the recursive rule s --> s,conj,s at the end of the knowledge base, so that Prolog always encounters the translation of the non-recursive rule first. What happens now, when we pose the query s([a,woman,shoots],[])? Well, now Prolog handles this and gives an answer. But what happens when we pose the query s([woman,shoot],[])? Note that this is an ungrammatical sentence that is not accepted by our grammar. Once again, Prolog gets into an infinite loop. Since it is impossible to recognise [woman,shoot] as a sentence consisting of a noun phrase and a verb phrase, Prolog tries to analyse it with the rule s --> s,conj,s, and ends up in the same unending loop as before.

In short, we are having the same problems that we met when we discussed recursion, and rule and goal ordering, in Chapter 3. In a nutshell, s --> s,conj,s translates into a left-recursive rule, and that's bad news. Moreover, as we saw earlier, we *can't* fix such problems simply by tinkering with the rule ordering: the way out of such difficulties is to change the goal order of the recursive rule so that the recursive goal is not the first one in the body of the rule. That is, ideally we should rewrite the rule so that it is no longer left-recursive.

Nice idea, but unfortunately, it is not an option here. Why not? Because the order of the goals determines the order of the words in the sentence! It makes an important difference, for example, whether our grammar accepts *the woman shoots the man and the man shoots the woman* (s --> s,conj,s) or whether it accepts *and the woman shoots the man the man shoots the woman* (s --> conj,s,s).

But there is a way out. The standard solution is to introduce a new non-terminal symbol and rewrite the DCG. We could, for example, use the category simple_s for sentences without embedded sentences. Our grammar would then look like this:

```
s --> simple_s.
s --> simple_s conj s.
simple_s --> np,vp.
np --> det,n.
vp --> v,np.
```

```
vp --> v.
det --> [the].
det --> [a].
n --> [woman].
n --> [man].
v --> [shoots].
conj --> [and].
conj --> [or].
conj --> [but].
```

As you should check, Prolog doesn't get into infinite loops with this grammar as it did with the previous one, so from a computational perspective the solution is satisfactory. But it leaves something to be desired from a linguistic perspective. The DCG that looped was at least faithful to the linguistic intuitions about the structure of sentences made using *and*, *but*, and *or*. The new DCG imposes an additional layer of structure that is motivated by processing rather than linguistic considerations; we are no longer simply turning grammars into Prolog.

The moral is: DCGs aren't magic. They are a nice notation, but you can't expect to write down an arbitrary CFG as a DCG and have it run without problems. DCG rules are ordinary Prolog rules in disguise, and this means that you must pay attention to what your Prolog interpreter is going to do with them. And in particular, you have to keep an eye out for left-recursion.

A DCG for a simple formal language

As our last example, we shall define a DCG for the formal language $a^n b^n$. What is this language? And what is a formal language anyway?

A formal language is simply a set of strings. The term "formal language" is intended to contrast with the term "natural language": whereas natural languages are languages that human beings actually use, formal languages are mathematical objects that computer scientists, logicians, and mathematicians define and study for various purposes.

A simple example of a formal language is $a^n b^n$. The words in this language are built up from two symbols: the symbol a and the symbol b. In fact, the language $a^n b^n$ consists of all strings made up from these two symbols that have the following form: the string must consist of an unbroken block of as of length n, followed by an unbroken block of bs of length n, and nothing else. So the strings ab, $aabb$, $aaabbb$ and $aaaabbbb$ all belong to $a^n b^n$. (Note that the empty string belongs to $a^n b^n$ too: after all, the empty string consists of a block of as of length zero followed by a block of *b*s of length zero.) On the other hand, *aba* and *abba* do not belong to $a^n b^n$.

Now, it is easy to write a context free grammar that generates this language:

$$
\begin{array}{l}
\text{s -> } \epsilon \\
\text{s -> l s r} \\
\text{l -> a} \\
\text{r -> b}
\end{array}
$$

The first rule says that an *s* can be realised as nothing at all. The second rule says that an *s* can be made up of an *l* (for left) element, followed by an *s*, followed by an *r* (for right) element. The last two rules say that *l* elements and *r* elements can be realised as *a*s and *b*s respectively. It should be clear that this grammar really does generate all and only the elements of $a^n b^n$, including the empty string.

Moreover, it is easy to turn this grammar into DCG. We can do so as follows:

```
s --> [].
s --> l,s,r.

l --> [a].
r --> [b].
```

Note that the second rule is recursive (but, thankfully, not left recursive). And in fact this DCG works exactly as we would hope. For example, to the query

```
?- s([a,a,a,b,b,b],[]).
```

we get the answer yes, while to the query

```
?- s([a,a,a,b,b,b,b],[]).
```

we get the answer no. The query

```
?- s(X,[]).
```

enumerates the strings in the language, starting from [].

3 Exercises

Exercise 7.1. Suppose we are working with the following DCG:

```
s --> foo,bar,wiggle.
foo --> [choo].
foo --> foo,foo.
bar --> mar,zar.
mar --> me,my.
me --> [i].
my --> [am].
zar --> blar,car.
blar --> [a].
car --> [train].
wiggle --> [toot].
wiggle --> wiggle,wiggle.
```

Write down the ordinary Prolog rules that correspond to these DCG rules. What are the first three responses that Prolog gives to the query s(X,[])?

Exercise 7.2. The formal language $a^n b^n - \{\epsilon\}$ consists of all the strings in $a^n b^n$ except the empty string. Write a DCG that generates this language.

Exercise 7.3. Let $a^n b^{2n}$ be the formal language which contains all strings of the following form: an unbroken block of *a*s of length n followed by an unbroken block of *b*s of length $2n$, and nothing else. For example, *abb*, *aabbbb*, and *aaabbbbbb* belong to $a^n b^{2n}$, and so does the empty string. Write a DCG that generates this language.

4 Practical Session

The purpose of this session is to help you get familiar with DCGs, difference lists, and the relation between them, and to give you some experience in writing basic DCGs. As you will learn in the following chapter, there is more to DCGs than the ideas just discussed. Nonetheless, what you have learned so far is certainly the core, and it is important that you are comfortable with the basic ideas before moving on.

First some keyboard exercises:

1. Type in or download the simple append/3 based recognisers discussed in the text, and then run some traces. As you will see, we were not exaggerating when we said that their performance is poor. Even for such simple sentences as *The woman shot a man* you will see that the traces are long and difficult to follow.

2. Next, type in or download our second recogniser, the one based on difference lists, and run more traces. As you will see, there is a

dramatic gain in efficiency. Moreover, you will see that the traces are *very* simple to understand, especially when compared with the monsters produced by the append/3 based implementations.

3. Next, type in or download the DCG discussed in the text. Type listing so that you can see what Prolog translates the rules to. How does your system translate rules of the form Det --> [the]? That is, does it translate them to rules like det([the|X],X), or does is make use of rules containing the 'C' predicate?

4. Now run some traces. Apart from variable names, the traces you observe here should be very similar to the traces you observed when running the difference list recogniser.

And now it's time to write some DCGs:

1. The formal language *Even* is very simple: it consists of all strings containing an even number of *a*s, and nothing else. Note that the empty string ϵ belongs to *Even*. Write a DCG that generates *Even*.

2. The formal language $a^n b^{2m} c^{2m} d^n$ consists of all strings of the following form: an unbroken block of *a*s followed by an unbroken block of *b*s followed by an unbroken block of *c*s followed by an unbroken block of *d*s, such that the *a* and *d* blocks are exactly the same length, and the *c* and *d* blocks are also exactly the same length and furthermore consist of an even number of *c*s and *d*s respectively. For example, ϵ, *abbccd*, and *aabbbbccccdd* all belong to $a^n b^{2m} c^{2m} d^n$. Write a DCG that generates this language.

3. The language that logicians call "propositional logic over the propositional symbols *p*, *q*, and *r*" can be defined by the following context free grammar:

$$
\begin{array}{l}
\texttt{prop -> p} \\
\texttt{prop -> q} \\
\texttt{prop -> r} \\
\texttt{prop -> } \neg \texttt{ prop} \\
\texttt{prop -> (prop } \wedge \texttt{ prop)} \\
\texttt{prop -> (prop } \vee \texttt{ prop)} \\
\texttt{prop -> (prop } \rightarrow \texttt{ prop)}
\end{array}
$$

Write a DCG that generates this language. Actually, because we don't know about Prolog operators yet, you will have to make a few rather clumsy looking compromises. For example, instead of getting it to recognise

$$\neg(p \ \rightarrow \ q)$$

you will have to get it recognise things like

```
[not, '(', p, implies, q, ')']
```

instead. We will learn in Chapter 9 how to deal with propositional logic somewhat more naturally; in the meantime, write a DCG that accepts a clumsy looking version of this language. Use *or* for ∨, and *and* for ∧.

Chapter 8

More Definite Clause Grammars

This chapter has two main goals:

1. To examine two important capabilities offered by DCG notation: extra arguments and extra tests.

2. To discuss the status and limitations of DCGs.

1 Extra Arguments

In the previous chapter we introduced basic DCG notation. But DCGs offer more than we've seen so far. For a start, DCGs allow us to specify extra arguments. Extra arguments can be used for many purposes; we'll examine three.

Context free grammars with features

As a first example, let's see how extra arguments can be used to add *features* to context-free grammars.

Here's the DCG we worked with in the previous chapter:

```
s --> np,vp.

np --> det,n.

vp --> v,np.
vp --> v.

det --> [the].
det --> [a].

n --> [woman].
n --> [man].

v --> [shoots].
```

Now, suppose we wanted to deal with sentences like "She shoots him", and "He shoots her". What should we do? Well, obviously we should add rules saying that "he", "she", "him", and "her" are pronouns:

```
pro --> [he].
pro --> [she].
pro --> [him].
pro --> [her].
```

Furthermore, we should add a rule saying that noun phrases can be pronouns:

```
np --> pro.
```

In this new DCG any good? Well, up to a point, it works. For example:

```
?- s([she,shoots,him],[]).
yes
```

But there's an obvious problem. The DCG will also accept a lot of sentences that are clearly wrong, such as "A woman shoots she", "Her shoots a man", and "Her shoots she":

```
?- s([a,woman,shoots,she],[]).
yes

?- s([her,shoots,a,man],[]).
yes

?- s([her,shoots,she],[]).
yes
```

That is, the grammar doesn't know that "she" and "he" are *subject* pronouns and cannot be used in *object* position; thus "A woman shoots she" is bad because it violates this basic fact about English. Moreover, the grammar doesn't know that "her" and "him" are *object* pronouns and cannot be used in *subject* position; thus "Her shoots a man" is bad because it violates this constraint. As for "Her shoots she", this manages to get both matters wrong at once.

Now, it's pretty obvious *what* we have to do to put this right: we need to extend the DCG with information about which pronouns can occur in subject position and which in object position. The interesting question: *how* exactly are we to do this? First let's look at a naive way of correcting this, namely adding new rules:

```
s --> np_subject,vp.

np_subject --> det,n.
np_object  --> det,n.
np_subject --> pro_subject.
np_object  --> pro_object.

vp --> v,np_object.
vp --> v.

det --> [the].
det --> [a].

n --> [woman].
n --> [man].

pro_subject --> [he].
```

```
pro_subject --> [she].
pro_object --> [him].
pro_object --> [her].
```

```
v --> [shoots].
```

Now this solution "works". For example,

```
?- s([her,shoots,she],[]).
no
```

But neither computer scientists nor linguists would consider this a good solution. The trouble is, a small addition to the lexicon has led to quite a big change in the DCG. Let's face it: "she" and "her" (and "he" and "him") are the same in a lot of respects. But to deal with the property in which they differ (namely, in which position they can occur in sentences) we've had to make big changes to the grammar: in particular, we've doubled the number of noun phrase rules. If we had to make further changes (for example, to cope with plural noun phrases) things would get even worse. What we really need is a more delicate programming mechanism that allows us to cope with such facts without being forced to add rules all the time. And here's where the extra arguments come into play. Look at the following grammar:

```
s --> np(subject),vp.
```

```
np(_) --> det,n.
np(X) --> pro(X).
```

```
vp --> v,np(object).
vp --> v.
```

```
det --> [the].
det --> [a].
```

```
n --> [woman].
n --> [man].
```

```
pro(subject) --> [he].
pro(subject) --> [she].
pro(object) --> [him].
pro(object) --> [her].
```

```
v --> [shoots].
```

The key thing to note is that this new grammar contains only one new noun phrase rule. In fact, it is very similar to the first grammar that we wrote, except that now the symbol np is associated with a new argument, either subject, object, _ or X. A linguist would say that we've added features to distinguish various kinds of noun phrase. In particular, note the four rules for the pronouns. Here we've used the extra argument to state which pronouns can occur in subject position, and which can occur in object position. Thus these rules are the most fundamental, for they give us the basic facts about how these pronouns can be used.

So what do the other rules do? Well, intuitively, the rule

```
np(X) --> pro(X).
```

uses the extra argument (the variable X) to pass these basic facts about pronouns up to noun phrases built out of them: because the variable X is used as the extra argument for both the np and the pronoun, Prolog unification will guarantee that they will be given the same value. In particular, if the pronoun we use is "she" (in which case X=subject), then the np will (through its extra argument X=subject) be marked as a subject np. On the other hand, if the pronoun we use is "her" (in which case X=object), then the extra argument for np will be marked X=object too. And this, of course, is exactly the behaviour we want.

On the other hand, although noun phrases built using the rule

```
np(_) --> det,n.
```

also have an extra argument, we've used the anonymous variable as its value. Essentially this means *can be either*, which is correct, for expressions built using this rule (such as "the man" and "a woman") can be used in both subject and object position.

Now consider the rule

```
vp --> v,np(object).
```

This says that to apply this rule we need to use a noun phrase whose extra argument unifies with object. This can be *either* noun phrases built from object pronouns *or* noun phrases such as "the man" and "a woman" which have the anonymous variable as the value of the extra argument. Crucially, pronouns marked has having subject as the value of the extra argument *can't* be used here: the atoms object and subject don't unify. Note that the rule

```
s --> np(subject),vp.
```

works in an analogous fashion to prevent noun phrases made of object
pronouns from ending up in subject position.

This works. You can check it out by posing the query:

```
?- s(X,[]).
```

As you step through the responses, you'll see that only acceptable
English is generated.

But while the intuitive explanation just given is correct, what's *really*
going on? The key thing to remember is that DCG rules are just a
convenient abbreviation. For example, the rule

```
s --> np,vp.
```

is really syntactic sugar for

```
s(A,B) :-
    np(A,C),
    vp(C,B).
```

That is, as we learned in the previous chapter, the DCG notation is
a way of hiding the two arguments responsible for the difference list
representation, so that we don't have to think about them. We work with
the nice user-friendly notation, and Prolog translates it into the clauses
just given.

Ok, so we obviously need to ask what

```
s --> np(subject),vp.
```

translates into. Here's the answer:

```
s(A,B) :-
    np(subject,A,C),
    vp(C,B).
```

As should now be clear, the name "extra argument" is a good one:
as this translation makes clear, the subject symbol really *is* just one
more argument in an ordinary Prolog rule. Similarly, our noun phrase
DCG rules translate into

```
np(A,B,C) :-
    det(B,D),
    n(D,C).
np(A,B,C) :-
    pro(A,B,C).
```

Note that both rules have *three* arguments. The first, A, is the extra argument, and the last two are the ordinary, hidden DCG arguments (the two hidden arguments are always the last two arguments).

Incidentally, how do you think we would use the grammar to list the grammatical noun phrases? Well, if we had been working with the DCG rule np --> det,n (that is, a rule with no extra arguments) we would have made the query

```
?- np(NP,[]).
```

So, in view of what we have just learned about extra arguments, it's not too surprising that we need to pose the query

```
?- np(X,NP,[]).
```

when working with our new DCG. And here's what the response would be:

```
X = _2625
NP = [the,woman] ;

X = _2625
NP = [the,man] ;

X = _2625
NP = [a,woman] ;

X = _2625
NP = [a,man] ;

X = subject
NP = [he] ;

X = subject
NP = [she] ;

X = object
NP = [him] ;

X = object
NP = [her] ;

no
```

One final remark: don't be misled by this simplicity of our example grammar. Extra arguments can be used to cope with some complex syntactic problems. DCGs are no longer the state-of-the-art grammar development tools they once were, but they're not toys either. Once you know about writing DCGs with extra arguments, you can write some fairly sophisticated grammars.

Building parse trees

So far, the programs we have discussed have been able to *recognise* grammatical structure (that is, they could correctly answer yes or no when asked whether the input was a sentence, a noun phrase, and so on) and to *generate* grammatical output. This is pleasant, but we would also like to be able to *parse*. That is, we would like our programs not only to tell us *which* sentences are grammatical, but also to give us an analysis of their structure. In particular, we would like to see the trees the grammar assigns to sentences.

Well, using only standard Prolog tools we can't actually draw nice pictures of trees, but we *can* build data structures which describe trees in a clear way. For example, corresponding to the tree

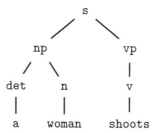

we could have the following term:

```
s(np(det(a),n(woman)),vp(v(shoots))).
```

Sure: it doesn't *look* as nice, but all the information in the picture is there. And, with the aid of a decent graphics package, it would be easy to turn this term into a picture.

But how do we get DCGs to build such terms? Actually, it's pretty easy. After all, in effect a DCG has to work out what the tree structure is when recognising a sentence. So we just need to find a way of keeping track of the structure that the DCG finds. We do this by adding extra arguments. Here's how:

```
s(s(NP,VP)) --> np(NP),vp(VP).
```

```
np(np(DET,N)) --> det(DET),n(N).

vp(vp(V,NP)) --> v(V),np(NP).
vp(vp(V))    --> v(V).

det(det(the)) --> [the].
det(det(a))   --> [a].

n(n(woman)) --> [woman].
n(n(man))   --> [man].

v(v(shoots)) --> [shoots].
```

What's going on here? Essentially we are building the parse trees for the syntactic categories on the left hand side of the rules out of the parse trees for the syntactic categories on the right hand side of the rules. Consider the rule vp(vp(V,NP)) --> v(V),np(NP). When we make a query using this DCG, the V in v(V) and the NP in np(NP) will be instantiated to terms representing parse trees. For example, perhaps V will be instantiated to

```
v(shoots)
```

and NP will be instantiated to

```
np(det(a),n(woman)).
```

What is the term corresponding to a vp made out of these two structures? Obviously it should be this:

```
vp(v(shoots),np(det(a),n(woman))).
```

And this is precisely what the extra argument vp(V,NP) given in the rule vp(vp(V,NP)) --> v(V),np(NP) returns to us: a term whose functor is vp, and whose first and second arguments are the values of V and NP respectively. To put it informally: it plugs the V and the NP terms together under a vp functor.

To parse the sentence "A woman shoots" we pose the query:

```
?- s(T,[a,woman,shoots],[]).
```

That is, we ask for the extra argument T to be instantiated to a parse tree for the sentence. And we get:

```
T = s(np(det(a),n(woman)),vp(v(shoots)))
yes
```

Furthermore, we can generate all parse trees by making the following query:

```
?- s(T,S,[]).
```

The first three responses are:

```
T = s(np(det(the),n(woman)),
       vp(v(shoots),np(det(the),n(woman)))))
S = [the,woman,shoots,the,woman] ;

T = s(np(det(the),n(woman)),
       vp(v(shoots),np(det(the),n(man)))))
S = [the,woman,shoots,the,man] ;

T = s(np(det(the),n(woman)),
       vp(v(shoots),np(det(a),n(woman)))))
S = [the,woman,shoots,a,woman]
```

In short, we have just seen an elegant (and useful) example of how to build structure using unification.

semantic representa- tions

Extra arguments can also be used to build semantic representations. Now, we did not say anything about what the words in our little DCG mean. In fact, nowadays a lot is known about the semantics of natural languages, and it is surprisingly easy to build semantic representations which partially capture the meaning of sentences or even entire discourses. Such representations are usually expressions of some formal language (for example first-order logic, discourse representation structures, or a database query language) and they are usually built up

compositio- nally

compositionally. That is, the meaning of each word is expressed in the formal language; this meaning is given as an extra argument in the DCG entries for the individual words. Then, for each rule in the grammar, an extra argument shows how to combine the meaning of the two subcomponents. For example, to the rule s --> np, vp we would add an extra argument stating how to combine the np meaning and the vp meaning to form the s meaning. Although somewhat more complex, the semantic construction process is quite like the way we built up the parse tree for the sentence from the parse tree of its subparts.[1]

---

[1] For a detailed account of how to do this, see *Representation and Inference for Natural Language: A First Course in Computational Semantics*, Patrick Blackburn and Johan Bos, CSLI Publications, 2005.

Beyond context free languages

In the previous chapter we introduced DCGs as a useful Prolog tool for representing and working with context free grammars. Now, this is certainly a good way of thinking about DCGs, but it's not the whole story. For the fact of the matter is: DCGs can deal with a lot more than just context free languages. The extra arguments we have been discussing (and indeed, the extra tests we shall introduce shortly) give us the tools for coping with any computable language whatsoever. We shall illustrate this by presenting a simple DCG for the formal language $a^n b^n c^n \backslash \{\epsilon\}$.

The formal language $a^n b^n c^n \backslash \{\epsilon\}$ consists of all non-null strings made up of as, bs, and cs which consist of an unbroken block of as, followed by an unbroken block of bs, followed by an unbroken block of cs, all three blocks having the same length. For example, abc, and aabbcc and aaabbbccc all belong to $a^n b^n c^n \backslash \{\epsilon\}$.

The interesting thing about this language is that it is *not* context free. Try whatever you like, you will not succeed in writing a context free grammar that generates precisely these strings. Proving this would take us too far afield, but the proof is not particularly difficult, and you can find it in many books on formal language theory.

On the other hand, as we shall now see, it is very easy to write a DCG that generates this language. Just as we did in the previous chapter, we shall represent strings as lists; for example, the string abc will be represented using the list [a,b,c]. Given this convention, here's the DCG we need:

```
s(Count) --> ablock(Count),bblock(Count),cblock(Count).

ablock(0) --> [].
ablock(succ(Count)) --> [a],ablock(Count).

bblock(0) --> [].
bblock(succ(Count)) --> [b],bblock(Count).

cblock(0) --> [].
cblock(succ(Count)) --> [c],cblock(Count).
```

The idea underlying this DCG is fairly simple: we use an extra argument to keep track of the length of the blocks. The s rule simply says that we want a block of as followed by a block of bs followed by block of cs, and all three blocks are to have the same length, namely Count.

What should the values of Count be? The obvious answer is: 1, 2, 3, 4, and so on. But as yet we don't know how to mix DCGs and arithmetic, so this isn't very helpful. Fortunately, as this DCG shows, there's an easier (and more elegant) way. Represent the number 0 by 0, the number 1 by succ(0), the number 2 by succ(succ(0)), the number 3 by succ(succ(succ(0))), and so on, just as we did it in Chapter 3 (as we said in Chapter 3, you can read succ as "successor of"). This choice of notation enables us to count using unification.

And this is precisely what our new DCG does. For example, suppose we pose the following query:

```
?- s(Count,L,[]).
```

which asks Prolog to generate the lists L of symbols that belong to this language, and to give the value of Count needed to produce each item. Then the first four responses are:

```
Count = 0
L = [] ;

Count = succ(0)
L = [a, b, c] ;

Count = succ(succ(0))
L = [a, a, b, b, c, c] ;

Count = succ(succ(succ(0)))
L = [a, a, a, b, b, b, c, c, c]
```

The value of Count clearly corresponds to the length of the blocks.

So: DCGs are not just a tool for working with context free grammars. They are strictly more powerful than that, and (as we've just seen) part of the extra power comes from the use of extra arguments.

2   Extra Goals

Any DCG rule is really syntactic sugar for an ordinary Prolog rule. So it's not really too surprising that we're allowed to make use of extra arguments. Similarly, it shouldn't come as too much of a surprise that we can call any Prolog predicate whatsoever from the right hand side of a DCG rule.

The DCG of the previous section can, for example, be adapted to work with Prolog numbers (instead of the successor representation of numbers) by using calls to Prolog's built-in arithmetic functionality. We simply count how many as, bs, and cs have been generated. Here's the code:

```
s --> ablock(Count),bblock(Count),cblock(Count).

ablock(0) --> [].
ablock(NewCount) --> [a],ablock(Count),
                     {NewCount is Count + 1}.

bblock(0) --> [].
bblock(NewCount) --> [b],bblock(Count),
                     {NewCount is Count + 1}.

cblock(0) --> [].
cblock(NewCount) --> [c],cblock(Count),
                     {NewCount is Count + 1}.
```

As this example suggests, extra goals can be written (anywhere) on the right side of a DCG rule, but must be placed between curly brackets. When Prolog encounters such curly brackets while translating a DCG into its internal representation, it just takes the extra goals specified between the curly brackets over into the translation. So, the second rule for the non-terminal ablock above would be translated as follows:

```
ablock(NewCount,A,B):-
   'C'(A, a, C),
   ablock(Count, C, B),
   NewCount is Count + 1.
```

Incidentally, if you play around with this DCG, you will find that there are actually some problems with it. In contrast to the one that we saw in the last section, this new version only works correctly when used in the recognition mode. If you try to generate with it, it will at some point enter an infinite loop. We won't bother to fix this problem here (apart from anything else, we find the earlier succ based approach more elegant).

The possibility of adding arbitrary Prolog goals to the right hand side of DCG rules, makes DCGs very powerful (it means that we can do anything that we can do in plain Prolog). In general, however, this capability is not used much, which tends to suggest that the basic DCG notation is well designed. There is, however, one classic application for extra goals in computational linguistics: with the help of extra goals, we can neatly separate grammar rules and lexical information. Let's see how.

Separating rules and lexicon

We are going to separate rules and lexicon. That is, we are going to eliminate all mention of individual words in our DCGs and instead record all the information about individual words separately in a lexicon. To see what is meant by this, let's return to our basic grammar:

```
np --> det,n.

vp --> v,np.
vp --> v.

det --> [the].
det --> [a].

n --> [woman].
n --> [man].

v --> [shoots].
```

We are now going to write a DCG that generates exactly the same language, but in which no rule mentions any individual word. All the information about individual words will be recorded separately.

Here is an example of a (very simple) lexicon. Lexical entries are encoded by using a predicate lex/2 whose first argument is a word, and whose second argument is a syntactic category.

```
lex(the,det).
lex(a,det).
lex(woman,n).
lex(man,n).
lex(shoots,v).
```

And here is a simple grammar that could go with this lexicon. In essence it's the same as the previous one. In fact, the only rules that have changed are those that mentioned specific words, that is, the det, n, and v rules.

```
np --> det,n.

vp --> v,np.
vp --> v.

det --> [Word],{lex(Word,det)}.
```

```
n --> [Word],{lex(Word,n)}.
v --> [Word],{lex(Word,v)}.
```

Consider the new det rule. This rule part says "a det can consist of a list containing a single element Word" (note that Word is a variable). Then the extra test adds the crucial stipulation: "so long as Word unifies with something that is listed in the lexicon as a determiner". With our present lexicon, this means that Word must be matched either with the word "a" or "the". So this single rule replaces the two previous DCG rules for det.

This explains the "how" of separating rules from lexicon, but it doesn't explain the "why". Is it really so important? Is this new way of writing DCGs really that much better?

The answer is an unequivocal yes! It's *much* better, and for at least two reasons.

The first reason is theoretical. Arguably rules should not mention specific lexical items. The purpose of rules is to list *general* syntactic facts, such as the fact that sentence can be made up of a noun phrase followed by a verb phrase. The rules for s, np, and vp describe such general syntactic facts, but the old rules for det, n, and v don't. Instead, the old rules simply list particular facts: that "a" is a determiner, that "the" is a determiner, and so on. From theoretical perspective it is much neater to have a single rule that says "anything is a determiner (or a noun, or a verb, or any other grammatical category) if it is listed as such in the lexicon". And this, of course, is precisely what our new DCG rules say.

The second reason is more practical. One of the key lessons computational linguists have learnt over the last twenty or so years is that the lexicon is by far the most interesting, important (and expensive!) repository of linguistic knowledge. Bluntly, if you want to get to grips with natural language from a computational perspective, you need to know a lot of words, and you need to know a lot about them.

Now, our little lexicon, with its simple two-place lex entries, is a toy. But a real lexicon is (most emphatically!) not. A real lexicon is likely to be very large (it may contain hundreds of thousands of words) and moreover, the information associated with each word is likely to be very rich. Our lex entries give only the syntactical category of each word, but a real lexicon will give much more, such as information about its phonological, morphological, semantic, and pragmatic properties.

Because real lexicons are big and complex, from a software engineering perspective it is best to write simple grammars that have a simple, well-defined way, of pulling out the information they need from vast lexicons. That is, grammars should be thought of as separate entities which can access the information contained in lexicons. We can then use specialised mechanisms for efficiently storing the lexicon and retrieving data from it.

Our new DCG rules, though simple, illustrate the basic idea. The new rules really do just list general syntactic facts, and the extra tests act as an interface to our lexicon that lets the rules find exactly the information they need. Furthermore, we now take advantage of Prolog's first argument indexing which makes looking up a word in the lexicon more efficient. First argument indexing is a technique for making Prolog's knowledge base access more efficient. If in the query the first argument is instantiated it allows Prolog to ignore all clauses where the first argument's functor and arity is different. This means, for example, that we can get all the possible categories of man immediately without having to even look at the lexicon entries for all the other hundreds or thousands of words that we might have in our lexicon.

first argument indexing

3   Concluding Remarks

We now have a fairly useful picture of what DCGs are and what they can do for us. To conclude, let's think about them from a somewhat higher level, from both a formal and a linguistic perspective.

First the formal remarks. For the most part, we have presented DCGs as a simple tool for encoding context free grammars (or context free grammars enriched with features such as *subject* and *object*). But DCGs go beyond this. We saw that it was possible to write a DCG that generated a language that was not context free. In fact, *any program whatsoever* can be written in DCG notation. That is, DCGs are a full-fledged programming language in their own right (they are Turing-complete, to use the proper terminology). And although DCGs are usually associated with linguistic applications, they can be useful for other purposes.

How good are DCGs from a linguistic perspective? Well, mixed. At one stage (in the early 1980s) they were pretty much state of the art. They made it possible to code complex grammars in a clear way, and to explore the interplay of syntactic and semantic ideas. Certainly any history of parsing in computational linguistics would give DCGs an honourable mention.

Nonetheless, DCGs have drawbacks. For a start, their tendency to loop when the goal ordering is wrong (we saw an example in the previous chapter when we added a left-recursive rule for conjunctions) is annoying; we *don't* want to think about such issues when writing serious grammars. Furthermore, while the ability to add extra arguments is useful, if we need to use lots of them (and for big grammars we will) it is a rather clumsy mechanism.

It is important to notice, however, that these problems come up because of the way Prolog interprets DCG rules. They are not inherent to the DCG notation. Any of you who have studied parsing algorithms probably know that all top-down parsers loop on left-recursive grammars. So, it is not surprising that Prolog, which interprets DCGs in a top-down fashion, loops on the left-recursive grammar rule s --> s conj s. If we used a different strategy to interpret DCGs, for example a bottom-up strategy, we would not run into the same problem. Similarly, if we didn't use Prolog's built-in interpretation of DCGs, we could use the extra arguments for a more sophisticated specification of features, one that would facilitate the use of large feature structures.

Summing up, nowadays DCGs are probably best viewed as a nice notation for defining context free grammars enhanced with some features, a notation that (ignoring left-recursion) doubles as a parser/recogniser. That is, they are best viewed as a convenient tool for testing new grammatical ideas, or for implementing reasonably complex grammars for particular applications. DCGs are no longer state of the art, but they are useful. Even if you have never programmed before, simply by using what you have learned so far you are ready to start experimenting with reasonably sophisticated grammar writing. With a conventional programming language (such as C++ or Java) it simply wouldn't be possible to reach this stage so soon. Things would be easier in functional languages (such as Lisp, Caml, or Haskell), but even so, it is doubtful whether beginners could do so much so early.

4   Exercises

Exercise 8.1.   Here's our basic DCG:

```
s --> np,vp.

np --> det,n.

vp --> v,np.
vp --> v.

det --> [the].
det --> [a].
```

```
n --> [woman].
n --> [man].
n --> [apple].
n --> [pear].

v --> [eat].
```

Suppose we add the noun "men" (which is plural) and the verb "know". Then we would want a DCG which says that "The men eat" is ok, "The man eats" is ok, "The men eats" is not ok, and "The man eat" is not ok. Change the DCG so that it correctly handles these sentences. Use an extra argument to cope with the singular/plural distinction.

Exercise 8.2.   In the text, we only gave examples of DCG rules with one extra argument, but in fact you can add as many extra arguments as you like. Here's a DCG rule with three extra arguments:

```
kanga(V,R,Q) --> roo(V,R),jumps(Q,Q),{marsupial(V,R,Q)}.
```

Translate it into the form Prolog uses.

5   Practical Session

The purpose of Practical Session 8 is to help you get familiar with DCGs that make use of additional arguments and tests.
    First some keyboard exercises:

1. Trace some examples using the DCG which uses extra arguments to handle the subject/object distinction, the DCG which produces parses, and the DCG which uses extra tests to separate lexicon and rules. Make sure you fully understand the way all three DCGs work.

2. Carry out traces on the DCG for $a^n b^n c^n$ given in the text (the one that gave the Count variable the values 0, succ(0), succ(succ(0)), and so on). Try cases where the three blocks of as, bs, and cs are indeed of the same length as well as queries where this is not the case.

Now for some programming. We suggest the following mini-project, which draws on all you have learned so far. Incidentally, in the Practical Session at the end of Chapter 12 we will be asking to extend this work even further, so do take this project seriously.

1. First, bring together all the things we have learned about DCGs for English into one DCG. In particular, in the text we saw how to use extra arguments to deal with the subject/object distinction, and in the exercises you were asked to use additional arguments to deal with the singular/plural distinction. Write a DCG which handles both. Moreover, write the DCG in such a way that it will produce parse trees, and makes use of a separate lexicon.

2. Once you have done this, extend the DCG so that noun phrases can be modified by adjectives and simple prepositional phrases (that is, it should be able to handle noun phrases such as "the small frightened woman on the table" or "the big fat cow under the shower"). Then, further extend it so that the distinction between first, second, and third person pronouns is correctly handled (both in subject and object form).

Chapter 9

A Closer Look at Terms

This chapter has three main goals:

1. To introduce the == predicate.

2. To take a closer look at term structure.

3. To introduce operators.

1 Comparing Terms

Prolog contains an important predicate for comparing terms, namely the identity predicate ==/2. As its name suggests, this tests whether two terms are identical. However ==/2 does *not* instantiate variables, thus it is not the same as the unification predicate =/2. Let's look at some examples.

```
?- a == a.
yes

?- a == b.
no

?- a == 'a'.
yes
```

identity predicate

The reason Prolog gives these answers should be clear, though pay attention to the last one. It tells us that, as far as Prolog is concerned, a and 'a' are the same object.

Now let's look at examples involving variables, and explicitly compare == with the unification predicate =.

```
?- X==Y.
no

?- X=Y.
X = _2808
Y = _2808
yes
```

In these queries, X and Y are *uninstantiated* variables; we haven't given them any value. Thus the first answer is correct: X and Y are *not* identical objects, so the == test fails. On the other hand, the use of = succeeds, for X and Y can be unified.

Let's now look at queries involving *instantiated* variables:

```
?- a=X, a==X.

X = a
yes
```

The first conjunct, a=X, binds X to a. Thus when a==X is evaluated, the left hand side and right hand sides are exactly the same Prolog object, and a==X succeeds.

A similar thing happens in the following query:

```
?- X=Y, X==Y.

X = _4500
Y = _4500
yes
```

The conjunct X=Y first unifies the variables X and Y. Thus when the second conjunct X==Y is evaluated, the two variables are exactly the same Prolog object, and the second conjunct succeeds as well.

It should now be clear that = and == are different, nonetheless there is an important relation between them: == can be viewed as a stronger test for equality between terms than =. That is, if term1 and term are Prolog terms, and the query term1 == term2 succeeds, then the query term1 = term2 will succeed too.

Another predicate worth knowing about is \==. This predicate is defined so that it succeeds in precisely those cases where == fails. That is, it succeeds whenever two terms are *not* identical, and fails otherwise. For example:

```
?- a \== a.
no

?- a \== b.
yes

?- a \== 'a'.
no
```

These answers should be understandable: they are simply the opposite of the answers we got above when we used ==. Now consider:

```
?- X \== a.

X = _3719
yes
```

Why this response? Well, we know from above that the query X==a *fails* (recall the way == treats uninstantiated variables). Thus the query X\==a should *succeed*, and it does.

Similarly:

```
?- X \== Y.

X = _798
Y = _799
yes
```

Again, we know from above that the query X==Y fails, thus the query X\==Y succeeds.

2   Terms with a Special Notation

Sometimes terms look different to us, but Prolog regards them as identical. For example, when we compare a and 'a', we see two distinct strings of symbols, but Prolog treats them as the same. And in fact there are many other cases where Prolog regards two strings as being exactly the same term. Why? Because it makes programming more pleasant. Sometimes the notation Prolog likes isn't as user-friendly as the notation we would choose. So it is nice to be able to write programs in the notation we find natural, and to let Prolog run them in the notation it prefers.

Arithmetic terms

The arithmetic predicates introduced earlier are a good example of this. As was mentioned in Chapter 5, +, -, *, and / are *functors*, and arithmetic expressions such as 2+3 are *terms*. And this is not an analogy. Apart from the fact that it can evaluate them with the help of the is/2 predicate, Prolog views strings of symbols such as 2+3 as being identical with ordinary complex terms. The following queries make this clear:

```
?- 2+3 == +(2,3).
yes

?- +(2,3) == 2+3.
yes

?- 2-3 == -(2,3).
yes

?- *(2,3) == 2*3.
yes

?- 2*(7+2) == *(2,+(7,2)).
yes
```

In short, the familiar arithmetic notation is there for *our* convenience. Prolog doesn't regard it as different from the usual term notation.

Similar remarks to the arithmetic comparison predicates <, =<, =:=, =\=, > and >=:

```
?- (2 < 3) == <(2,3).
yes

?- (2 =< 3) == =<(2,3).
yes

?- (2 =:= 3) == =:=(2,3).
yes

?- (2 =\= 3) == =\=(2,3).
yes

?- (2 > 3) == >(2,3).
yes

?- (2 >= 3) == >=(2,3).
yes
```

These example show why it's nice to have the user-friendly notation (would you want to have to work with expressions like =:=(2,3)?). Note, by the way, that we enclosed the left hand arguments in brackets. For example, we didn't ask

```
?- 2 =:= 3 == =:=(2,3).
```

we asked

```
?- (2 =:= 3) == =:=(2,3).
```

Why? Well, Prolog finds the query 2 =:= 3 == =:=(2,3) confusing, and let's face it, can you blame it? It's not sure whether to bracket this expression as (2 =:= 3) == =:=(2,3) (which is what we want), or as 2 =:= (3 == =:=(2,3)). So we need to state the grouping explicitly.

One final remark. We have now introduced three rather similar looking symbols, namely =, ==, and =:= (and indeed, there are also \=, \==, and =\=). Here's a summary:

=   The unification predicate.

Succeeds if it can unify its arguments, fails otherwise.

\\=   The negation of the unification predicate.

Succeeds if = fails, and vice-versa.

==   The identity predicate.

Succeeds if its arguments are identical, fails otherwise.

\\==   The negation of the identity predicate.

Succeeds if == fails, and vice-versa.

=:=   The arithmetic equality predicate.

Succeeds if its arguments evaluate to the same integer.

=\\=   The arithmetic inequality predicate.

Succeeds if its arguments evaluate to different integers.

Lists as terms

Lists are another good example of Prolog working with one internal representation, while giving us another, more user-friendly, notation to work with. Let's start with a quick look at the user-friendly list notation it provides (that is, the square brackets [and]). In fact, because Prolog also offers the | constructor, there are many ways of writing the same list, even at the user-friendly level:

```
?- [a,b,c,d] == [a|[b,c,d]].
yes


?- [a,b,c,d] == [a,b|[c,d]].
yes


?- [a,b,c,d] == [a,b,c|[d]].
yes


?- [a,b,c,d] == [a,b,c,d|[]].
yes
```

But how does Prolog view lists internally? In fact, it sees lists as terms which are built out of two special terms, namely [], which represents the empty list, and "." (the full-stop), a functor of arity 2 which is used to build non-empty lists. The terms [] and . are called list constructors.

list con-
structors

This is how these constructors are used to build lists. Needless to say, the definition is recursive:

- The empty list is the term [ ]. It has length 0.

- A non-empty list is any term of the form .(*term*, *list*), where *term* is any Prolog term, and *list* is any list. If *list* has length n, then .(*term*, *list*) has length $n + 1$.

Let's make sure we fully understand this definition by working our way through a few examples.

```
?- .(a,[]) == [a].
yes

?- .(f(d,e),[]) == [f(d,e)].
yes

?- .(a,.(b,[])) == [a,b].
yes

?- .(a,.(b,.(f(d,e),[]))) == [a,b,f(d,e)].
yes

?- .(.(a,[]),[]) == [[a]].
yes

?- .(.(.(a,[]),[]),[]) == [[[a]]].
yes

?- .(.(a,.(b,[])),[]) == [[a,b]].
yes

?- .(.(a,.(b,[])),.(c,[])) == [[a,b],c].
yes

?- .(.(a,[]),.(b,.(c,[]))) == [[a],b,c].
yes

?- .(.(a,[]),.(.(b,.(c,[])),[])) == [[a],[b,c]].
yes
```

Prolog's internal notation for lists is not as user-friendly as the use of the square bracket notation. But it's not as bad as it seems at first sight. In fact, it works similarly to the | notation. It represents a list in two parts: its first element (the head), and a list representing the rest of the list (the tail). The trick is to read these terms as *trees*. The internal nodes of this tree are labeled with . and all have two daughter nodes. The subtree under the left daughter represents the first element of the list and the subtree under the right daughter represents the rest of the list. For example, the tree representation of .(a,.(.(b,.(c,[])),.(d,[]))), that is, [a, [b,c], d], looks like this:

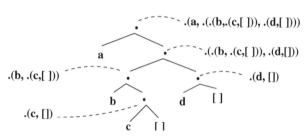

One final remark. Prolog is very polite. Not only are you free to talk to it in the user-friendly notation, it will reply in the same way:

```
?- .(f(d,e),[]) = Y.

Y = [f(d,e)]
yes


?- .(a,.(b,[])) = X, Z= .(.(c,[]),[]), W = [1,2,X].

X = [a,b]
Z = [[c]]
W = [1,2,[a,b]]
yes
```

3 Examining Terms

In this section, we will learn about some built-in predicates that let us examine terms more closely. First, we will look at predicates that test whether their arguments are terms of a certain type (for example, whether they are atoms or numbers). Then we will introduce predicates that tell us something about the internal structure of complex terms.

Types of Terms

Remember what we said about Prolog terms in Chapter 1: there are four different kinds, namely variables, atoms, numbers and complex terms. Furthermore, atoms and numbers are grouped together under the name constants, and constants and variables constitute the simple terms. The following tree diagram summarises this:

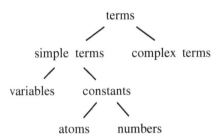

Sometimes it is useful to be able to determine what type a given term is. You might, for example, want to write a predicate that has to deal with different kinds of terms, but has to treat them in different ways. Prolog provides several built-in predicates that test whether a given term is of a certain type:

atom/1   Is the argument an atom?
integer/1   Is the argument an integer?
float/1   Is the argument a floating point number?
number/1   Is the argument an integer or a floating point number?
atomic/1   Is the argument a constant?
var/1   Is the argument an uninstantiated variable?
nonvar/1   Is the argument an instantiated variable or another term
            that is not an *un*instantiated variable?

Let's see how they behave.

```
?- atom(a).
yes

?- atom(7).
no

?- atom(loves(vincent,mia)).
no
```

These three examples behave exactly as we would expect. But what happens, when we call atom/1 with a variable as argument?

```
?- atom(X).
no
```

This makes sense, since an uninstantiated variable is not an atom. However if we instantiate X with an atom first and then ask atom(X), Prolog answers yes.

```
?- X = a, atom(X).
X = a
yes
```

But it is important that the instantiation is done *before* the test:

```
?- atom(X), X = a.
no
```

The predicates integer/1 and float/1 behave analogously. Try some examples.

The predicates number/1 and atomic/1 behave disjunctively. First, number/1 tests whether a given term is either an integer or a float: that is, it will evaluate to true whenever either integer/1 or float/1 evaluate to true and it fails when both of them fail. As for atomic/1, this tests whether a given term is a constant, that is, whether it is either an atom or a number. So atomic/1 will evaluate to true whenever either atom/1 or number/1 evaluate to true and it fails when both fail.

```
?- atomic(mia).
yes

?- atomic(8).
yes

?- atomic(3.25).
yes

?- atomic(loves(vincent,mia)).
no

?- atomic(X)
no
```

What about variables? First there is the var/1 predicate. This tests whether the argument is an *uninstantiated* variable:

```
?- var(X)
yes
```

```
?- var(mia).
no

?- var(8).
no

?- var(3.25).
no

?- var(loves(vincent,mia)).
no
```

Then there is the nonvar/1 predicate. This succeeds precisely when var/1 fails; that is, it tests whether its argument is *not* an uninstantiated variable:

```
?- novar(X)
no

?- nonvar(mia).
yes

?- nonvar(8).
yes

?- nonvar(3.25).
yes

?- nonvar(loves(vincent,mia)).
yes
```

Note that a complex term which contains uninstantiated variables is not itself an uninstantiated variable (it is a complex term). Therefore we have:

```
?- var(loves(_,mia)).
no

?- nonvar(loves(_,mia)).
yes
```

And when the variable X gets instantiated var(X) and nonvar(X) behave differently depending on whether they are called before or after the instantiation:

```
?- X = a, var(X).
no

?- X = a, nonvar(X).
X = a
yes

?- var(X), X = a.
X = a
yes

?- nonvar(X), X = a.
no
```

The Structure of Terms

Given a complex term of unknown structure (perhaps a complex term returned as the output of some predicate), what kind of information might we want to extract from it? The obvious response is: its functor, its arity, and what its arguments look like. Prolog provides built-in predicates that provide this information. Information about the functor and arity is supplied by the predicate functor/3. Given a complex term, functor/3 will tell us what its functor and arity are:

```
?- functor(f(a,b),F,A).
A = 2
F = f
yes

?- functor([a,b,c],X,Y).
X = '.'
Y = 2
yes
```

Note that when asked about a list, Prolog returns the functor ., which is the functor it uses in its internal representation of lists.

What happens when we use functor/3 with constants? Let's try:

```
?- functor(mia,F,A).
A = 0
F = mia
yes
```

```
?- functor(8,F,A).
A = 0
F = 8
yes

?- functor(3.25,F,A).
A = 0
F = 3.25
yes
```

So we can use the predicate `functor/3` to find out the functor and the arity of a term, and this usage also works for the special case of 0 arity terms (constants).

We can also use `functor/3` to *construct* terms. How? By specifying the second and third argument and leaving the first undetermined. The query

```
?- functor(T,f,7).
```

for example, returns the following answer:

```
T = f(_G286, _G287, _G288, _G289, _G290, _G291, _G292)
yes
```

Note that either the first argument or the second and third argument have to be instantiated. For example, Prolog would answer with an error message to the query `functor(T,f,N)`. And if you think about what the query means, Prolog is reacting in a sensible way. The query is asking Prolog to construct a complex term without telling it how many arguments to provide, which is not a very sensible request.

Now that we know about `functor/3`, let's put it to work. In the previous section, we discussed the built-in predicates that tested whether their argument was an atom, a number, a constant, or a variable. But there was no predicate that tested whether its argument was a complex term. To make the list complete, let's define such a predicate. It is easy to do so using `functor/3`. All we have to do is to check that there is a suitable functor, and that the input has arguments (that is, that its arity is greater than zero). Here is the definition:

```
complexterm(X):-
    nonvar(X),
    functor(X,_,A),
    A > 0.
```

So much for functors — what about arguments? In addition to the predicate functor/3, Prolog supplies us with the predicate arg/3 which tells us about the arguments of complex terms. It takes a number N and a complex term T and returns the *Nth* argument of T in its third argument. It can be used to access the value of an argument

```
?- arg(2,loves(vincent,mia),X).
X = mia
yes
```

or to instantiate an argument

```
?- arg(2,loves(vincent,X),mia).
X = mia
yes
```

Trying to access an argument which doesn't exist, of course, fails:

```
?- arg(2,happy(yolanda),X).
no
```

The predicates functor/3 and arg/3 allow us to access all the basic information we need to know about complex terms. However Prolog also supplies a third built-in predicate for analysing term structure, namely '=..'/2. This takes a complex term and returns a list that has the functor as its head, and then all the arguments, in order, as the elements of the tail. So to the query

```
?- '=..'(loves(vincent,mia),X)
```

Prolog will respond

```
X = [loves,vincent,mia]
```

univ This predicate (which is called univ) can also be used as an infix operator. Here are some examples showing various ways of using this (very useful) tool:

```
?- cause(vincent,dead(zed)) =.. X.
X = [cause, vincent, dead(zed)]
yes

?- X =.. [a,b(c),d].
X = a(b(c), d)
yes
```

```
?- footmassage(Y,mia) =.. X.
Y = _G303
X = [footmassage, _G303, mia]
yes
```

Univ really comes into its own when something has to be done to all arguments of a complex term. Since it returns the arguments as a list, normal list processing strategies can be used to traverse the arguments.

Strings

Strings are represented in Prolog by a list of character (ASCII) codes. However, it would be a right kerfuffle to use list notation for simple string manipulation, so Prolog also offers a user-friendly notation for strings: double quotes. Try the following query:

```
?- S = "Vicky".
S = [86, 105, 99, 107, 121]
yes
```

Here the variable S unifies with the string "Vicky", which is a list containing of five numbers, each of them corresponding to the character codes of the single characters the strings is composed of. (For instance, 86 is the character code for the character V, 105 is the code for the character i, and so on.)

In other words, strings in Prolog are actually lists of numbers. Several standard predicates are supported by most Prolog dialects to work with strings. A particularly useful one is atom_codes/2. This predicate converts an atom into a string. The following examples illustrate what atom_codes/2 can do for you:

```
?- atom_codes(vicky,X).
X = [118, 105, 99, 107, 121]
yes

?- atom_codes('Vicky',X).
X = [86, 105, 99, 107, 121]
yes

?- atom_codes('Vicky Pollard',X).
X = [86, 105, 99, 107, 121, 32, 80, 111, 108|...]
yes
```

It also works the other way around: atom_codes/2 can also be used to generate atoms from strings. Suppose you want to duplicate an atom abc into the atom abcabc. This is how you could do it:

```
?- atom_codes(abc,X), append(X,X,L), atom_codes(N,L).

X = [97, 98, 99]
L = [97, 98, 99, 97, 98, 99]
N = abcabc
```

One last thing you need to know about the atom_codes/2 predicate is that it is related to another other built-in predicate, namely number_codes/2. This predicate behaves in a similar way, but, as the names suggest, only works for numbers.

4   Operators

As we have seen, in certain cases (for example, when performing arithmetic) Prolog lets us use operator notations that are more user-friendly than its own internal representations. Indeed, as we shall now see, Prolog even has a mechanism for letting us define our own operators. In this section we'll first take a closer look at the properties of operators, and then learn how to define our own.

Properties of operators

Let's start with an example from arithmetic. Internally, Prolog uses the expression is(11,+(2,*(3,3))), but we are free to write the functors * and + between their arguments, to form the more user-friendly expression 11 is 2 + 3 * 3. Functors that can be written between their arguments

infix operators

are called infix operators. Other examples of infix operators in Prolog are :-, -->, ;, ',', =, =.., == and so on. In addition to infix

prefix operators

operators there are also prefix operators (which are written before their arguments) and postfix operators (which are written after). For example,

postfix operators

?- is a prefix operator, and so is the one-place - which is used to represent negative numbers (as in 1 is 3 + -2). An example of a postfix operator is the ++ notation used in the C programming language to increment the value of a variable.

When we learned about arithmetic in Prolog, we saw that Prolog knows about the conventions for disambiguating arithmetic expressions. So when we write 2 + 3 * 3, Prolog knows that we mean 2 + (3 * 3) and not (2 + 3) * 3. But how does Prolog know this? Because

precedence

every operator has a certain precedence. The precedence of + is greater than the precedence of *, and that's why + is taken to be the main functor of the expression 2 + 3 * 3. (Note that Prolog's internal representation +(2,*(3,3)) is not ambiguous.) Similarly, the precedence of is is higher than the precedence of +, so 11 is 2 + 3 * 3 is interpreted as is(11,+(2,*(3,3))) and not as the (nonsensical) expression +(is(11,2),*(3,3)). In Prolog, precedence is expressed by a number between 0 and 1200; the higher the number, the greater the precedence. To give some examples, the precedence of = is 700, the precedence of + is 500, and the precedence of * is 400.

What happens when there are several operators with the same precedence in one expression? We said above that Prolog finds the query 2 =:= 3 == =:=(2,3) confusing. It doesn't know how to bracket the expression: Is it =:=(2,==(3,=:=(2,3))) or is it ==(=:=(2,3),=:=(2,3))? The reason Prolog is not able to decide on the correct bracketing is because == and =:= have the same precedence. In such cases, explicit bracketings must be supplied by the programmer.

What about the following query though?

    ?- X is 2 + 3 + 4.

Does Prolog find this confusing? Not at all: it deals with it happily and correctly answers X = 9. But which bracketing did Prolog choose: is(X,+(2,+(3,4))) or is(X,+(+(2,3),4))? As the following queries show, it chose the second:

    ?- 2 + 3 + 4 = +(2,+(3,4)).
    no
    ?- 2 + 3 + 4 = +(+(2,3),4).
    yes

Here Prolog has used information about the associativity of + to disambiguate: + is left associative, which means that the expression to the right of + must have a lower precedence than + itself, whereas the expression on the left may have the same precedence as +. The precedence of an expression is simply the precedence of its main operator, or 0 if it is enclosed in brackets. The main operator of 3 + 4 is +, so that interpreting 2 + 3 + 4 as +(2,+(3,4)) would mean that the expression to the right of the first + has the same precedence as + itself, which is illegal. It has to be lower.

The operators ==, =:=, and is are defined to be non-associative, which means that both of their arguments must have a lower precedence. Therefore 2 =:= 3 == =:=(2,3) is an illegal expression, since no matter how you bracket it you'll get a conflict: 2 =:= 3 has the same precedence as ==, and 3 == =:=(2,3) has the same precedence as =:=.

associativity

left associative

non-associative

The type of an operator (infix, prefix, or postfix), its precedence, and its associativity are the three things that Prolog needs to know to be able to translate user-friendly (but potentially ambiguous) operator notations into Prolog's internal representation.

Defining operators

In addition to providing a user-friendly operator notation for certain functors, Prolog also lets you define your own operators. So you could, for example, define a postfix operator is_dead; then Prolog would allow you to write zed is_dead as a fact in your database instead of is_dead(zed).

Operator definitions in Prolog look like this:

```
:- op(Precedence,Type,Name).
```

As we mentioned above, precedence is a number between 0 and 1200, and the higher the number, the greater the precedence. Type is an atom specifying the type and associativity of the operator. In the case of + this atom is yfx, which says that + is an infix operator; the f represents the operator, and the x and y the arguments. Furthermore, x stands for an argument which has a precedence which is lower than the precedence of + and y stands for an argument which has a precedence which lower or equal to the precedence of +. There are the following possibilities for type:

infix	xfx, xfy, yfx
prefix	fx, fy
suffix	xf, yf

So your operator definition for is_dead might be as follows:

```
:- op(500, xf, is_dead).
```

Here are the definitions for some of the built-in operators. You can see that operators with the same properties can be specified in one statement by giving a list of their names (instead of a single name) as the third argument of op.

```
:- op( 1200, xfx, [ :-, --> ]).
:- op( 1200,  fx, [ :-, ?- ]).
:- op( 1100, xfy, [ ; ]).
:- op( 1000, xfy, [ ',' ]).
:- op(  700, xfx, [ =, is, =.., ==, \==,
                    =:=, =\=, <, >, =<, >= ]).
:- op(  500, yfx, [ +, -]).
:- op(  500,  fx, [ +, - ]).
:- op(  300, xfx, [ mod ]).
:- op(  200, xfy, [ ^ ]).
```

One final point should made explicit. Operator definitions don't specify the *meanings* of operators, they only describe how they can be used syntactically. That is, an operator definition doesn't say anything about when a query involving this operator will evaluate to true, it merely extends the *syntax* of Prolog. So if the operator is_dead is defined as above, and you pose the query zed is_dead, Prolog won't complain about illegal syntax (as it would without this definition) but will try to prove the goal is_dead(zed), which is Prolog's internal representation of zed is_dead. And this is all operator definitions do — they just tell Prolog how to translate a user-friendly notation into real Prolog notation. So, what would be Prolog's answer to the query zed is_dead? It would be no, because Prolog would try to prove is_dead(zed), but would not find any matching clause in the database. But suppose we extended the database as follows:

```
:- op(500, xf, is_dead).

kill(Marcellus,zed).
is_dead(X) :- kill(_,X).
```

Now Prolog would answer yes to the query.

5 Exercises

Exercise 9.1.   Which of the following queries succeed, and which fail? $\boxed{\mathcal{E}}$

```
?- 12 is 2*6.
```

```
?- 14 =\= 2*6.
```

```
?- 14 = 2*7.
```

```
?- 14 == 2*7.

?- 14 \== 2*7.

?- 14 =:= 2*7.

?- [1,2,3|[d,e]] == [1,2,3,d,e].

?- 2+3 == 3+2.

?- 2+3 =:= 3+2.

?- 7-2 =\= 9-2.

?- p == 'p'.

?- p =\= 'p'.

?- vincent == VAR.

?- vincent=VAR, VAR==vincent.
```

Exercise 9.2. How does Prolog respond to the following queries?

```
?- .(a,.(b,.(c,[]))) = [a,b,c].

?- .(a,.(b,.(c,[]))) = [a,b|[c]].

?- .(.(a,[]),.(.(b,[]),.(.(c,[]),[]))) = X.

?- .(a,.(b,.(.(c,[]),[]))) = [a,b|[c]].
```

Exercise 9.3. Write a two-place predicate `termtype(Term,Type)` that takes a term and gives back the type(s) of that term (atom, number, constant, variable, and so on). The types should be given back in the order of their generality. The predicate should behave in the following way.

```
?- termtype(Vincent,variable).
yes
?- termtype(mia,X).
```

```
X = atom ;
X = constant ;
X = simple_term ;
X = term ;
no
?- termtype(dead(zed),X).
X = complex_term ;
X = term ;
no
```

Exercise 9.4.   Write a Prolog program that defines the predicate $\boxed{\mathcal{E}}$
groundterm(Term) which tests whether or not Term is a ground term.
Ground terms are terms that don't contain variables. Here are examples
of how the predicate should behave:

```
?- groundterm(X).
no
?- groundterm(french(bic_mac,le_bic_mac)).
yes
?- groundterm(french(whopper,X)).
no
```

Exercise 9.5.   Assume that we have the following operator definitions. $\boxed{\mathcal{E}}$

```
:- op(300, xfx, [are, is_a]).
:- op(300, fx, likes).
:- op(200, xfy, and).
:- op(100, fy, famous).
```

Which of the following are well-formed terms?   What are the main
operators? Give the bracketings.

```
X is_a witch
harry and ron and hermione are friends
harry is_a wizard and likes quidditch
dumbledore is_a famous wizard
```

6 Practical Session

To start this session, we'll introduce some built-in predicates for printing
terms onto the screen. You should try out the following examples as we
introduce them. The first predicate we want to look at is display/1.
Here are some simple examples:

```
?- display(loves(vincent,mia)).
loves(vincent, mia)

yes
?- display('jules eats a big kahuna burger').
jules eats a big kahuna burger

yes
```

But the really important point about display/1, as the following examples demonstrate, is that it prints Prolog's *internal representation* of terms to the screen:

```
?- display(2+3+4).
+(+(2, 3), 4)

yes
```

This property of display/1 makes it a very useful tool for learning how operators work in Prolog. So, before going on, try the following queries. Make sure you understand why Prolog answers the way it does.

```
?- display([a,b,c]).
?- display(3 is 4 + 5 / 3).
?- display(3 is (4 + 5) / 3).
?- display((a:-b,c,d)).
?- display(a:-b,c,d).
```

So display/1 is useful when we want to look at the internal representation of terms in operator notation. But often we would prefer to see the user-friendly notation instead. For example, when reading lists it is usually more pleasant to see [a,b,c] rather than .(a.(b.(c,[]))). The built-in predicate write/1 lets us view terms like this. This predicate takes a term and prints it to the screen in the user-friendly notation.

```
?- write(2+3+4).
2+3+4
yes

?- write(+(2,3)).
2+3
yes
```

```
?- write([a,b,c]).
[a, b, c]
yes

?- write(.(a,.(b,[]))).
[a, b]
yes
```

And here is what happens when the term to be written contains variables:

```
?- write(X).
_G204
X = _G204
yes

?- X = a, write(X).
a
X = a
yes
```

The following example shows what happens when you give two write/1 commands one after the other:

```
?- write(a),write(b).
ab

yes
```

That is, Prolog just executes one after the other without putting any space in between the output of the two commands. Of course, you can get Prolog to print space by telling it to write the term ' ':

```
?- write(a),write(' '),write(b).
a b

yes
```

And if you want more than one space, for example five blanks, you can tell Prolog to write '   '.

```
?- write(a),write('     '),write(b).
a     b

yes
```

Another way of printing spaces is by using the predicate `tab/1`. This takes a number as argument and then prints that number of spaces:

```
?- write(a),tab(5),write(b).
a     b

yes
```

Another predicate useful for formatting is `nl`. This tells Prolog to make a line-break and to go on printing on the next line.

```
?- write(a),nl,write(b).
a
b
yes
```

Time to apply what you have just learned. In the last chapter we saw how extra arguments in DCGs could be used to build parse trees. For example, to the query

```
s(T,[a,man,shoots,a,woman],[])
```

Prolog would answer

```
s(np(det(a),n(man)),vp(v(shoots),np(det(a),n(woman)))).
```

This term is a representation of the parse tree, but it is not a very readable representation. It would be nicer if Prolog printed something like the following (this style of printing is usually called pretty printing):

pretty
printing

```
s(
  np(
     det(a)
     n(man))
  vp(
     v(shoots)
     np(
        det(a)
        n(woman))))
```

Write a predicate `pptree/1` that takes a complex term representing a tree as its argument and prints the tree in a more readable form.

Time to practice writing operator definitions. In the practical session of Chapter 7, you were asked to write a DCG generating propositional logic formulas. The input you had to use was a bit awkward though. The formula $\neg(p \rightarrow q)$ had to be represented as [not, '(', p, implies, q, ')']. Now that you know about operators, you can do things rather more neatly. Write operator definitions for not, and, or, and implies, so that Prolog accepts (and correctly brackets) propositional logic formulas. Use display/1 to check your code. It should yield the following kinds of response:

```
?- display(not(p implies q)).
not(implies(p,q)).

yes

?- display(not p implies q).
implies(not(p),q)

yes
```

Chapter 10

Cuts and Negation

This chapter has two main goals:

1. To explain how to control Prolog's back-tracking behaviour with the help of the cut predicate.

2. To explain how cut can be packaged into a more structured form, namely negation as failure.

1   The Cut

Automatic backtracking is one of the most characteristic features of Prolog. But backtracking can lead to inefficiency. Sometimes Prolog can waste time exploring possibilities that lead nowhere. It would be pleasant to have some control over this aspect of its behaviour, but so far we have only seen two (rather crude) ways of doing this: changing rule order, and changing goal order. But there is another way. There is a built-in Prolog predicate ! (the exclamation mark), called cut, which offers a more direct way of exercising control over the way Prolog looks for solutions.

cut

What exactly is cut, and what does it do? It's simply a special atom that we can use when writing clauses. For example,

```
p(X):- b(X), c(X), !, d(X), e(X).
```

is a perfectly good Prolog rule. As for what cut does, first of all, it is a goal that *always* succeeds. Second, and more importantly, it has a side effect. Suppose that some goal makes use of this clause (we call this goal the parent goal). Then the cut commits Prolog to any choices that were made since the parent goal was unified with the left hand side of the rule (including, importantly, the choice of using that particular clause). Let's look at an example to see what this means.

First consider the following piece of cut-free code:

```
p(X):- a(X).

p(X):- b(X), c(X), d(X), e(X).

p(X):- f(X).

a(1).   b(1).    c(1).    d(2).   e(2).   f(3).
        b(2).    c(2).
```

If we pose the query p(X) we will get the following responses:

```
X = 1 ;

X = 2 ;

X = 3 ;
no
```

Here is the search tree that explains how Prolog finds these three solutions. Note that it has to backtrack once, namely when it enters the second clause for p/1 and decides to unify the first goal with b(1) instead of b(2).

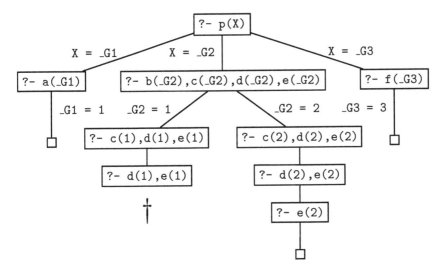

But now suppose we insert a cut in the second clause:

p(X):- b(X), c(X), !, d(X), e(X).

If we now pose the query p(X) we will get the following responses:

X = 1 ;
no

What's going on here? Let's consider.

1. p(X) is first unified with the first rule, so we get a new goal a(X). By instantiating X to 1, Prolog unifies a(X) with the fact a(1) and we have found a solution. So far, this is exactly what happened in the first version of the program.

2. We then go on and look for a second solution. p(X) is unified with the second rule, so we get the new goals b(X),c(X),!,d(X),e(X). By instantiating X to 1, Prolog unifies b(X) with the fact b(1), so we now have the goals c(1),!,d(1),e(1). But c(1) is in the database so this simplifies to !,d(1),e(1).

3. Now for the big change. The ! goal succeeds (as it always does) and commits us to the choices made so far. In particular, we are committed to having X = 1, and we are also committed to using the second rule.

4. But d(1) fails. And there's no way we can re-satisfy the goal
p(X). Sure, if we were allowed to try the value X=2 we could use
the second rule to generate a solution (that's what happened in the
original version of the program). But we *can't* do this: the cut
has removed this possibility from the search tree. And sure, if we
were allowed to try the third rule, we could generate the solution
X=3. But we *can't* do this: once again, the cut has removed this
possibility from the search tree.

If you look at the search tree, you'll see that this all boils down to
the following: search stops when the goal d(1) doesn't lead to any
node where an alternative choice is available. The crosses in the search
tree indicate the branches that the cut trimmed away.

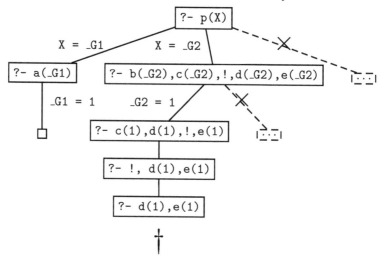

One point is worth emphasising: the cut only commits us to choices
made since the parent goal was unified with the left hand side of the
clause containing the cut. For example, in a rule of the form

    q:- p1,...,pn, !, r1,...,rm

when we reach the cut it commits us to using this particular clause for
q and it commits us to the choices made when evaluating p1,...,pn.
However, we *are* free to backtrack among the r1,...,rm and we are
also free to backtrack among alternatives for choices that were made
before reaching the goal q. A concrete example will make this clear.

First consider the following cut-free program:

```
s(X,Y):- q(X,Y).
s(0,0).

q(X,Y):- i(X), j(Y).

i(1).
i(2).

j(1).
j(2).
j(3).
```

Here's how it behaves:

```
?- s(X,Y).

X = 1
Y = 1 ;

X = 1
Y = 2 ;

X = 1
Y = 3 ;

X = 2
Y = 1 ;

X = 2
Y = 2 ;

X = 2
Y = 3 ;

X = 0
Y = 0;
no
```

And this is the corresponding search tree:

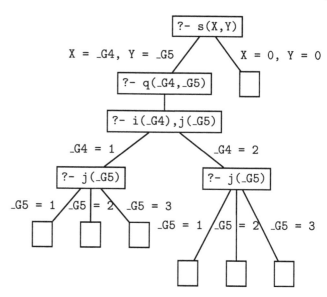

Suppose we add a cut to the clause defining q/2:

q(X,Y):- i(X), !, j(Y).

Now the program behaves as follows:

?- s(X,Y).

X = 1
Y = 1 ;

X = 1
Y = 2 ;

X = 1
Y = 3 ;

X = 0
Y = 0;
no

Let's see why.

1. s(X,Y) is first unified with the first rule, which gives us a new
   goal q(X,Y).

2. q(X,Y) is then unified with the third rule, so we get the new goals i(X),!,j(Y). By instantiating X to 1, Prolog unifies i(X) with the fact i(1). This leaves us with the goal !,j(Y). The cut, of course, succeeds, and commits us to the choices made so far.

3. But what are these choices? These: that X = 1, and that we are using this clause. But note: we have *not* yet chosen a value for Y.

4. Prolog then goes on, and by instantiating Y to 1, Prolog unifies j(Y) with the fact j(1). So we have found a solution.

5. But we can find more. Prolog *is* free to try another value for Y. So it backtracks and sets Y to 2, thus finding a second solution. And in fact it can find another solution: on backtracking again, it sets Y to 3, thus finding a third solution.

6. But those are all alternatives for j(X). Backtracking to the left of the cut is not allowed, so it *can't* reset X to 2, so it won't find the next three solutions that the cut-free program found. Backtracking over goals that were reached before q(X,Y) is allowed however, so that Prolog will find the second clause for s/2.

Here's the corresponding search tree:

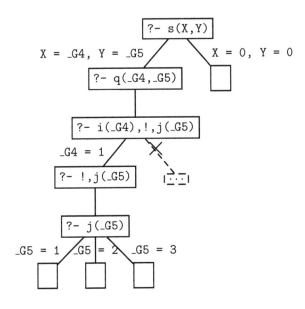

2   Using Cut

Well, we now know what cut is. But how do we use it in practice, and why is it so useful? As a first example, let's define a (cut-free) predicate max/3 which takes integers as arguments and succeeds if the third argument is the maximum of the first two. For example, the queries

```
?- max(2,3,3).
```

and

```
?- max(3,2,3).
```

and

```
?- max(3,3,3).
```

should succeed, and the queries

```
?- max(2,3,2).
```

and

```
?- max(2,3,5).
```

should fail. And of course, we also want the program to work when the third argument is a variable. That is, we want the program to be able to find the maximum of the first two arguments for us:

```
?- max(2,3,Max).

Max = 3
yes

?- max(2,1,Max).

Max = 2
yes
```

Now, it is easy to write a program that does this. Here's a first attempt:

```
max(X,Y,Y):- X =< Y.
max(X,Y,X):- X>Y.
```

This is a perfectly correct program, and we might be tempted simply to stop here. But we shouldn't: it's not good enough.

What's the problem? There is a potential inefficiency. Suppose this definition is used as part of a larger program, and somewhere along the way max(3,4,Y) is called. The program will correctly set Y=4. But now consider what happens if at some stage backtracking is forced. The program will try to re-satisfy max(3,4,Y) using the second clause. This is completely pointless: the maximum of 3 and 4 is 4 and that's that. There is no second solution to find. To put it another way: the two clauses in the above program are mutually exclusive: if the first succeeds, the second must fail and vice versa. So attempting to re-satisfy this clause is a complete waste of time.

With the help of cut, this is easy to fix. We need to insist that Prolog should never try both clauses, and the following code does this:

```
max(X,Y,Y) :- X =< Y,!.
max(X,Y,X) :- X>Y.
```

Note how this works. Prolog will reach the cut if max(X,Y,Y) is called and X =< Y succeeds. In this case, the second argument is the maximum, and that's that, and the cut commits us to this choice. On the other hand, if X =< Y fails, then Prolog goes onto the second clause instead.

Note that this cut does *not* change the meaning of the program. Our new code gives exactly the same answers as the old one, but it's more efficient. In fact, the program is *exactly* the same as the previous version, except for the cut, and this is a pretty good sign that the cut is a sensible one. Cuts like this, which don't change the meaning of a program, have a special name: they're called green cuts.

green cuts

But some readers will dislike this code. After all, isn't the second line redundant? If we have to use this line, we already know that the first argument is bigger that the second. Couldn't we squeeze out a little more efficiency with the help of our new cut construct? Let's try. Here's a first (faulty) attempt:

```
max(X,Y,Y) :- X =< Y,!.
max(X,Y,X).
```

Note that is the same as our earlier green cut max/3, except that we have got rid of the > test in the second clause. How good is it? Well, for some queries it's fine. In particular, it answers correctly when we pose queries in which the third argument is a variable. For example:

```
?- max(100,101,X).
```

```
X = 101
yes
```

and

```
?- max(3,2,X).
```

```
X = 3
yes
```

Nonetheless, it's *not* the same as the green cut program: the new max/3 does *not* work correctly. Consider what happens when all three arguments are instantiated. For example, consider the query

```
?- max(2,3,2).
```

Obviously this query should fail. But in our new version, it will succeed! Why? Well, this query simply won't unify with the head of the first clause, so Prolog goes straight to the second clause. And the query will unify with the second clause, and (trivially) the query succeeds! So maybe getting rid of that > test wasn't quite so smart after all.

But there is another way. The problem with the new code is simply that we carried out variable unification *before* we traversed the cut. Suppose we handle our variables a little more intelligently (using three variables instead of two) and explicitly unify *after* we have crossed the cut:

```
max(X,Y,Z) :- X =< Y,!, Y = Z.
max(X,Y,X).
```

As the reader should check, this program does work, and (as we hoped for) it avoids the explicit comparison made in the second clause of our green cut version of max/3.

But there is an important difference between the new version of the program and the green cut version. The cut in the new program is a classic example of what is known as a **red cut**. As this terminology is supposed to suggest, such cuts are potentially dangerous. Why? Because if we take out such a cut, we *don't* get an equivalent program. That is, if we remove the cut, the resulting code does *not* compute the maximum of two numbers any more. To put it another way, the presence of the cut is *indispensable* to the correct functioning of the program. (This was not the case in the green cut version — the cut there merely improved efficiency.) Because red cuts are indispensable cuts, their presence means that programs containing them are not fully declarative. Now, red cuts can be useful on occasions, but beware! Their use can lead to subtle programming mistakes and make code hard to debug.

So, what to do? It's probably best to work as follows. Try and get a good, clear, cut-free program working, and only then try to improve its efficiency by using cuts. Use green cuts whenever possible. Red cuts should be used only when absolutely necessary, and it's a good idea to explicitly comment on any red cuts in your code. Working this way will maximise your chances of striking a good balance between declarative clarity and procedural efficiency.

3 Negation as Failure

One of Prolog's most useful features is the simple way it lets us state generalisations. To say that Vincent enjoys burgers we just write:

```
enjoys(vincent,X) :- burger(X).
```

But in real life rules have exceptions. Perhaps Vincent doesn't like Big Kahuna burgers. That is, perhaps the correct rule is really: Vincent enjoys burgers, *except* Big Kahuna burgers. Fine. But how do we state this in Prolog?

As a first step, let's introduce another built-in predicate: fail/0. As its name suggests, fail/0 is a special symbol that will immediately fail when Prolog encounters it as a goal. That may not sound too useful, but remember: *when Prolog fails, it tries to backtrack.* Thus fail/0 can be viewed as an instruction to force backtracking. And when used in combination with cut, which *blocks* backtracking, fail/0 enables us to write some interesting programs, and in particular, it lets us define exceptions to general rules.

Consider the following code:

```
enjoys(vincent,X) :- big_kahuna_burger(X),!,fail.
enjoys(vincent,X) :- burger(X).

burger(X) :- big_mac(X).
burger(X) :- big_kahuna_burger(X).
burger(X) :- whopper(X).

big_mac(a).
big_kahuna_burger(b).
big_mac(c).
whopper(d).
```

The first two lines describe Vincent's preferences. The last six lines describe a world containing four burgers, a, b, c, and d. We're also given information about what kinds of burgers they are. Given that the first two lines really do describe Vincent's preferences (that is, that he likes all burgers except Big Kahuna burgers) then he should enjoy burgers a, c and d, but not b. And indeed, this is what happens:

```
?- enjoys(vincent,a).
yes

?- enjoys(vincent,b).
no

?- enjoys(vincent,c).
yes

?- enjoys(vincent,d).
yes
```

cut-fail
combina-
tion

How does this work? The key is the combination of ! and fail/0 in the first line (this even has a name: it's called the cut-fail combination). When we pose the query enjoys(vincent,b), the first rule applies, and we reach the cut. This commits us to the choices we have made, and in particular, blocks access to the second rule. But then we hit fail/0. This tries to force backtracking, but the cut blocks it, and so our query fails.

This is interesting, but it's not ideal. For a start, note that the ordering of the rules is crucial: if we reverse the first two lines, we *don't* get the behaviour we want. Similarly, the cut is crucial: if we remove it, the program doesn't behave in the same way (so this is a *red* cut). In short, we've got two mutually dependent clauses that make intrinsic use of the procedural aspects of Prolog. Something useful is clearly going on here, but it would be better if we could extract the useful part and package it in a more robust way.

And we can. The crucial observation is that the first clause is essentially a way of saying that Vincent does *not* enjoy X if X is a Big Kahuna burger. That is, the cut-fail combination seems to be offering us some form of negation. And indeed, this is the crucial generalisation: the cut-fail combination lets us define a form of negation called negation

negation as
failure

as failure. Here's how:

```
neg(Goal) :- Goal,!,fail.
neg(Goal).
```

For any Prolog goal, neg(Goal) will succeed precisely if Goal does *not* succeed.

Using our new neg/1 predicate, we can describe Vincent's preferences in a much clearer way:

```
enjoys(vincent,X) :- burger(X),
                     neg(big_kahuna_burger(X)).
```

That is, Vincent enjoys X if X is a burger and X is not a Big Kahuna burger. This is quite close to our original statement: Vincent enjoys burgers, except Big Kahuna burgers.

Negation as failure is an important tool. Not only does it offer useful expressivity (notably, the ability to describe exceptions) it also offers it in a relatively safe form. By working with negation as failure (instead of with the lower level cut-fail combination) we have a better chance of avoiding the programming errors that often accompany the use of red cuts. In fact, negation as failure is so useful that it comes built-in as part of standard Prolog, so we don't have to define it at all. In standard Prolog the operator \+ means negation as failure, so we could define Vincent's preferences as follows:

```
enjoys(vincent,X) :- burger(X),
                     \+ big_kahuna_burger(X).
```

Nonetheless, a couple of words of warning are in order: *don't* make the mistake of thinking that negation as failure works just like logical negation. It doesn't. Consider again our burger world:

```
burger(X) :- big_mac(X).
burger(X) :- big_kahuna_burger(X).
burger(X) :- whopper(X).

big_mac(c).
big_kahuna_burger(b).
big_mac(c).
whopper(d).
```

If we pose the query enjoys(vincent,X) we get the correct sequence of responses:

```
X = a ;

X = c ;

X = d ;
no
```

But now suppose we rewrite the first line as follows:

```
enjoys(vincent,X) :- \+ big_kahuna_burger(X), burger(X).
```

Note that from a declarative point of view, this should make no difference: after all, *burger(x) and not big kahuna burger(x)* is logically equivalent to *not big kahuna burger(x) and burger(x)*. That is, no matter what the variable *x* denotes, it is impossible for one of these expressions to be true and the other false. Nonetheless, here's what happens when we pose the same query:

```
?- enjoys(vincent,X).
```

```
no
```

What's going on? Well, in the modified database, the first thing that Prolog has to check is whether `\+ big_kahuna_burger(X)` holds, which means that it must check whether `big_kahuna_burger(X)` fails. But this succeeds. After all, the database contains the information `big_kahuna_burger(b)`. So the query `\+ big_kahuna_burger(X)` fails, and hence the original query does too. In a nutshell, the crucial difference between the two programs is that in the original version (the one that works right) we use `\+` only *after* we have instantiated the variable X. In the new version (which goes wrong) we use `\+` before we have done this. The difference is crucial.

Summing up, we have seen that negation as failure is not logical negation, and that it has a procedural dimension that must be understood. Nonetheless, it is an important programming construct: it is generally a better idea to try use negation as failure than to write code containing heavy use of red cuts. Nonetheless, "generally" does not mean "always". There *are* times when it is better to use red cuts.

For example, suppose that we need to write code to capture the following condition: *p holds if a and b hold, or if a does not hold and c holds too*. This can be captured with the help of negation as failure very directly:

```
p :- a,b.
```

```
p :- \+ a, c.
```

But suppose that a is a very complicated goal, a goal that takes a lot of time to compute. Programming it this way means we may have to compute a twice, and this may mean that we have unacceptably slow performance. If so, it would be better to use the following program:

```
p :- a,!,b.

p :- c.
```

Note that this is a red cut: removing it changes the meaning of the program.

When all's said and done, there are no universal guidelines that will cover all the situations you are likely to run across. Programming is as much an art as a science: that's what makes it so interesting. You need to know as much as possible about the language you are working with (whether it's Prolog, Java, Perl, or whatever), understand the problem you are trying to solve, and know what counts as an acceptable solution. And then: go ahead and try your best!

4 Exercises

Exercise 10.1. Suppose we have the following database: $\mathcal{E}$

```
p(1).
p(2) :- !.
p(3).
```

Write all of Prolog's answers to the following queries:

```
?- p(X).
```

```
?- p(X),p(Y).
```

```
?- p(X),!,p(Y).
```

Exercise 10.2. First, explain what the following program does: $\mathcal{E}$

```
class(Number,positive) :- Number > 0.
class(0,zero).
class(Number,negative) :- Number < 0.
```

Second, improve it by adding green cuts.

Exercise 10.3. Without using cut, write a predicate split/3 that splits $\mathcal{E}$ a list of integers into two lists: one containing the positive ones (and zero), the other containing the negative ones. For example:

```
split([3,4,-5,-1,0,4,-9],P,N)
```

should return:

```
P = [3,4,0,4]

N = [-5,-1,-9].
```

Then improve this program, without changing its meaning, with the help of the cut.

Exercise 10.4.

Recall that in Exercise 3.3 we gave you the following knowledge base:

```
directTrain(saarbruecken,dudweiler).
directTrain(forbach,saarbruecken).
directTrain(freyming,forbach).
directTrain(stAvold,freyming).
directTrain(fahlquemont,stAvold).
directTrain(metz,fahlquemont).
directTrain(nancy,metz).
```

We asked you to write a recursive predicate travelFromTo/2 that told us when we could travel by train between two towns.

Now, it's plausible to assume that whenever it is possible to take a direct train from A to B, it is also possible to take a direct train from B to A. Add this information to the database. Then write a predicate route/3 which gives you a list of towns that are visited by taking the train from one town to another. For instance:

```
?- route(forbach,metz,Route).
Route = [forbach,freyming,stAvold,fahlquemont,metz]
```

5 Practical Session

The purpose of this session is to help you get familiar with cuts and negation as failure. First some keyboard exercises:

1. Try out all three versions of the max/3 predicate defined in the text: the cut-free version, the green cut version, and the red cut version. As usual, "try out" means "run traces on", and you should make sure that you trace queries in which all three arguments are instantiated to integers, and queries where the third argument is given as a variable.

2. Ok, time for a burger. Try out all the methods discussed in the text for coping with Vincent's preferences. That is, try out the

program that uses a cut-fail combination, the program that uses negation as failure correctly, and also the program that mucks it up by using negation in the wrong place.

Now for some programming:

1. Define a predicate nu/2 ("not unifiable") which takes two terms as arguments and succeeds if the two terms do not unify. For example:

```
nu(foo,foo).
no

nu (foo,blob).
yes

nu(foo,X).
no
```

You should define this predicate in three different ways:

(a) First (and easiest) write it with the help of = and \+.

(b) Second write it with the help of =, but don't use \+.

(c) Third, write it using a cut-fail combination. Don't use = and don't use \+.

2. Define a predicate unifiable(List1,Term,List2) where List2 is the list of all members of List1 that unify with Term. The elements of List2 should *not* be instantiated by the unification. For example

```
unifiable([X,b,t(Y)],t(a),List]
```

should yield

```
List = [X,t(Y)].
```

Note that X and Y are still *not* instantiated. So the tricky part is: how do we check that they unify with t(a) without instantiating them?

(Hint: consider using tests of the form \+ term1 = term2. Why? Think about it. You might also like to think about tests of the form \+ \+ term1 = term2.)

Chapter 11

Database Manipulation and Collecting Solutions

This chapter has two main goals:

1. To discuss database manipulation in Prolog.

2. To discuss built-in predicates that let us collect all solutions to a problem into a single list.

1 Database Manipulation

assert
retract
asserta
assertz

Prolog has four database manipulation commands: assert, retract, asserta, and assertz. Let's see how these are used. Suppose we start with an empty database. So if we give the command:

```
?- listing.
```

then Prolog will simply respond yes; the listing (of course) is empty.
Suppose we now give this command:

```
?- assert(happy(mia)).
```

This succeeds (assert/1 commands *always* succeed). But what is important is not that it succeeds, but the side-effect it has on the database. For if we now give the command

```
?- listing.
```

we get:

```
happy(mia).
```

That is, the database is no longer empty: it now contains the fact we asserted.
Suppose we then made four more assert commands:

```
?- assert(happy(vincent)).
yes

?- assert(happy(marcellus)).
yes

?- assert(happy(butch)).
yes

?- assert(happy(vincent)).
yes
```

and then ask for a listing:

```
?- listing.

happy(mia).
happy(vincent).
happy(marcellus).
happy(butch).
happy(vincent).
yes
```

All the facts we asserted are now in the knowledge base. Note that
happy(vincent) is in the knowledge base twice. As we asserted it
twice, this seems sensible.

The database manipulations we have been making have changed the
meaning of the predicate happy/1. More generally, database manipulation
commands give us the ability to change the meaning of predicates while
we are running programs. Predicates whose definitions change during
run-time are called dynamic predicates, as opposed to the static predicates
that we have previously dealt with. Most Prolog interpreters insist that
we explicitly declare the predicates that we wish to be dynamic. We
will soon examine an example involving dynamic predicates, but let's
first complete our discussion of the database manipulation commands.

| dynamic |
| predicates |

| static |
| predicates |

So far we have only asserted facts into the database, but we can also
assert new rules. Suppose we want to assert the rule that everyone who
is happy is naive. That is, suppose we want to assert that:

```
naive(X):- happy(X).
```

We can do this as follows:

```
assert( (naive(X):- happy(X)) ).
```

Note the syntax of this command: *the rule we are asserting is enclosed
in a pair of brackets*. If we now ask for a listing we get:

```
happy(mia).
happy(vincent).
happy(marcellus).
happy(butch).
happy(vincent).

naive(A):-
    happy(A).
```

Now that we know how to assert new information into the database,
we should also learn how to remove information when we no longer
need it. There is an inverse predicate to assert/1, namely retract/1.
For example, if we carry straight on from the previous example by
giving the command:

```
?- retract(happy(marcellus)).
```

and then list the database, we get:

```
happy(mia).
happy(vincent).
happy(butch).
happy(vincent).

naive(A) :-
    happy(A).
```

That is, the fact happy(marcellus) has been removed.
Suppose we go on further, and say

```
?- retract(happy(vincent)).
```

and then ask for a listing. We get:

```
happy(mia).
happy(butch).
happy(vincent).

naive(A) :-
    happy(A).
```

Note that the first occurrence of happy(vincent), and *only* the first
occurrence, was removed.

To remove all of our assertions contributing to the definition of the
predicate happy/1 we can use a variable:

```
?- retract(happy(X)).

X = mia ;

X = butch ;

X = vincent ;
no
```

A listing reveals that the database is now empty, except for the rule
naive(A) :- happy(A).

```
?- listing.
naive(A) :-
    happy(A).
```

If we want more control over where the asserted material is placed, there are two variants of `assert/1`, namely:

1. assertz. Places asserted material at the *end* of the database. | assertz |

2. asserta. Places asserted material at the *beginning* of the database. | asserta |

For example, suppose we start with an empty database, and then we give the following command:

```
assert( p(b) ), assertz( p(c) ), asserta( p(a) ).
```

Then a listing reveals that we now have the following database:

```
?- listing.

p(a).
p(b).
p(c).
yes
```

Database manipulation is a useful technique. It is especially useful for storing the results to computations, so that if we need to ask the same question in the future, we don't need to redo the work: we just look up the asserted fact. This technique is called memoisation, or caching, and in some applications it can greatly increase efficiency. Here's a simple example of this technique at work: | memoisation | | caching |

```
:- dynamic lookup/3.

add_and_square(X,Y,Res):-
    lookup(X,Y,Res), !.

add_and_square(X,Y,Res):-
    Res is (X+Y)*(X+Y),
    assert(lookup(X,Y,Res)).
```

What does this program do? Basically, it takes two numbers X and Y, adds X to Y, and then squares the result. For example we have:

```
?- add_and_square(3,7,X).

X = 100
yes
```

But the important point is: *how* does it do this? First, note that we have declared `lookup/3` as a dynamic predicate. We need to do this as we plan to change the definition of `lookup/3` during run-time. Second, note that there are two clauses defining `add_and_square/3`. The second clause performs the required arithmetic calculation and asserts the result to the Prolog database using the predicate `lookup/3` (that is, it caches the result). The first clause checks the Prolog database to see if the calculation has already been made in the past. If it has been, the program simply returns the result, and the cut prevents it from entering the second clause.

Here's an example of the program at work. Suppose we give Prolog another query

```
?- add_and_square(3,4,Y).

Y = 49
yes
```

If we now ask for a listing we see that the database now contains

```
lookup(3, 7, 100).
lookup(3, 4, 49).
```

Should we later ask Prolog to add and square 3 and 4, it wouldn't perform the calculations again. Rather, it would just return the previously calculated result.

Question: how do we remove all these new facts when we no longer want them? After all, if we give the command

```
?- retract(lookup(X,Y,Z)).
```

Prolog will go through all the facts one by one and ask us whether we want to remove them! But there's a much simpler way. Simply use the command

```
?- retractall(lookup(_,_,_)).
```

This will remove all facts about `lookup/3` from the database.

To conclude our discussion of database manipulation, a word of warning. Although it is a useful technique, database manipulation can lead to dirty, hard to understand, code. If you use it heavily in a program with lots of backtracking, understanding what is going on can be a nightmare. It is a non-declarative, non logical, feature of Prolog that should be used cautiously.

2 Collecting Solutions

There may be many solutions to a query. For example, suppose we are working with the database

```
child(martha,charlotte).
child(charlotte,caroline).
child(caroline,laura).
child(laura,rose).

descend(X,Y) :- child(X,Y).

descend(X,Y) :- child(X,Z),
                descend(Z,Y).
```

Then if we pose the query

```
descend(martha,X).
```

there are four solutions (namely X=charlotte, X=caroline, X=laura, and X=rose).

However Prolog generates these solutions one by one. Sometimes we would like to have *all* the solutions to a query, and we would like them handed to us in a neat, usable, form. Prolog has three built-in predicates that do this: findall, bagof and setof. In essence, all these predicates collect all the solutions to a query and put them in a single list — but there are important differences between them, as we shall see.

findall

bagof

setof

The findall/3 predicate

The query

```
?- findall(Object,Goal,List).
```

produces a list List of all the objects Object that satisfy the goal Goal. Often Object is simply a variable, in which case the query can be read as: *Give me a list containing all the instantiations of* Object *which satisfy* Goal.

Here's an example. Suppose we're working with the above database (that is, with the information about child and the definition of descend). Then if we pose the query

```
?- findall(X,descend(martha,X),Z).
```

we are asking for a list Z containing all the values of X that satisfy descend(martha,X). Prolog will respond

```
X = _7489
Z = [charlotte,caroline,laura,rose]
```

But Object doesn't have to be a variable, it may be a complex term that just contains a variable that also occurs in Goal. For example, we might decide that we want to build a new predicate fromMartha/1 that is true only of descendants of Martha. We could do this with the query:

```
?- findall(fromMartha(X),descend(martha,X),Z).
```

That is, we are asking for a list Z containing all the instantiations of fromMartha(X) that satisfy the goal descend(martha,X). Prolog will respond

```
X = _7616
Z = [fromMartha(charlotte),fromMartha(caroline),
            fromMartha(laura),fromMartha(rose)]
```

What happens if we ask the following query?

```
?- findall(X,descend(mary,X),Z).
```

As there are no solutions for the goal descend(mary,X) in the knowledge base. findall/3 returns an empty list.

Note that the first two arguments of findall/3 typically have (at least) one variable in common. When using findall/3, we normally want to know what solutions Prolog finds for certain variables in the goal, and we tell Prolog which variables in Goal we are interested in by building them into the first argument of findall/3.

You might encounter situations, however, where findall/3 does useful work although the first two arguments don't share any variables. For example, if you are not interested in who exactly is a descendant of Martha, but only in how many descendants Martha has, you can use the following query to find out:

```
?- findall(Y,descend(martha,X),Z), length(Z,N).
```

The bagof/3 predicate

The findall/3 predicate is useful, but in certain respects it is rather crude. For example, suppose we pose the query

```
?- findall(Child,descend(Mother,Child),List).
```

We get the response

```
Child = _6947
Mother = _6951
List = [charlotte,caroline,laura,rose,caroline,
        laura,rose,laura,rose,rose]
```

Now, this is correct, but sometimes it would be useful if we had a separate list for each of the different instantiations of Mother.

This is what bagof/3 lets us do. If we pose the query

```
?- bagof(Child,descend(Mother,Child),List).
```

we get the response

```
Child = _7736
Mother = caroline
List = [laura,rose] ;

Child = _7736
Mother = charlotte
List = [caroline,laura,rose] ;

Child = _7736
Mother = laura
List = [rose] ;

Child = _7736
Mother = martha
List = [charlotte,caroline,laura,rose] ;
no
```

That is, bagof/3 is more fine-grained than findall/3. It gives us the opportunity to extract the information we want in a more structured way. Moreover, bagof/3 can also do the same job as findall/3, with the help of a special piece of syntax, namely ^:

```
?- bagof(Child,Mother^descend(Mother,Child),List).
```

This says: *give me a list of all the values of* Child *such that* descend(Mother,Child), *and put the result in a list, but don't worry about generating a separate list for each value of* Mother. So posing this query yields:

```
Child = _7870
Mother = _7874
List = [charlotte,caroline,laura,rose,caroline,
        laura,rose,laura,rose,rose]
```

Note that this is exactly the response that findall/3 would have given
us. Still, if this is the kind of query you want to make (and it often is)
it's simpler to use findall/3, because then you don't have to bother
explicitly write down the conditions using ˆ.

There is one important difference between findall/3 and bagof/3,
namely that bagof/3 fails if the goal that is specified in its second
argument is not satisfied (remember, that findall/3 returns the empty
list in such cases). So the query bagof(X,descend(mary,X),Z) yields
no.

One final remark. Consider again the query

```
?- bagof(Child,descend(Mother,Child),List).
```

As we saw above, this has four solutions. But, once again, Prolog
generates them one by one. Wouldn't it be nice if we could collect
them all into one list?

And we can. The simplest way is to use findall/3. The query

```
?- findall(List,
            bagof(Child,descend(Mother,Child),List),
            Z).
```

collects all of bagof/3's responses into one list:

```
List = _8293
Child = _8297
Mother = _8301
Z = [[laura,rose],[caroline,laura,rose],[rose],
                  [charlotte,caroline,laura,rose]]
```

Another way to do it is with bagof/3:

```
?- bagof(List,
         ChildˆMotherˆbagof(Child,descend(Mother,Child),List),
         Z).

List = _2648
Child = _2652
Mother = _2655
Z = [[laura,rose],[caroline,laura,rose],[rose],
                  [charlotte,caroline,laura,rose]]
```

This may not be the sort of thing you need to do very often, but it
does show the flexibility and power offered by these predicates.

The setof/3 **predicate**

The setof/3 predicate is basically the same as bagof/3, but with one useful difference: the lists it contains are *ordered* and contain *no redundancies* (that is, no list contains repeated items).

For example, suppose we have the following database

```
age(harry,13).
age(draco,14).
age(ron,13).
age(hermione,13).
age(dumbledore,60).
age(hagrid,30).
```

Now suppose we want a list of everyone whose age is recorded in the database. We can do this with the query:

```
?- findall(X,age(X,Y),Out).
```

```
X = _8443
Y = _8448
Out = [harry,draco,ron,hermione,dumbledore,hagrid]
```

But maybe we would like the list to be ordered. We can achieve this with the following query:

```
?- setof(X,Y^age(X,Y),Out).
```

(Note that, just as with bagof/3, we have to tell setof/3 not to generate separate lists for each value of Y, and again we do this with the ^ symbol.) This query yields:

```
X = _8711
Y = _8715
Out = [draco,dumbledore,hagrid,harry,hermione,ron]
```

Note that the list is alphabetically ordered.

Now suppose we are interested in collecting together all the ages which are recorded in the database. Of course, we could do this with the following query:

```
?- findall(Y,age(X,Y),Out).
```

```
Y = _8847
X = _8851
Out = [13,14,13,13,60,30]
```

But this output is rather messy. It is unordered and contains repetitions. By using setof/3 we get the same information in a neater form:

```
?- setof(Y,X^age(X,Y),Out).

Y = _8981
X = _8985
Out = [13,14,30,60]
```

Between them, these three predicates offer us a great deal of flexibility when it comes to collecting solutions. For many purposes, all we need is findall/3, but if we need more, bagof/3 and setof/3 are there waiting to help us out. But bear in mind that there is an important difference between findall/3 on the one hand and bagof/3 and setof/3 on the other: findall/3 will return an empty list if the goal has no solutions, whereas bagof/3 and setof/3 would fail in such a situation.

3   Exercises

Exercise 11.1.   Suppose we start with an empty database. We then give the command:

```
assert(q(a,b)), assertz(q(1,2)), asserta(q(foo,blug)).
```

What does the database now contain?
  We then give the command:

```
retract(q(1,2)), assertz( (p(X) :- h(X)) ).
```

What does the database now contain?
  We then give the command:

```
retractall(q(_,_)).
```

What does the database now contain?

Exercise 11.2.   Suppose we have the following database:

```
q(blob,blug).
q(blob,blag).
q(blob,blig).
q(blaf,blag).
q(dang,dong).
q(dang,blug).
q(flab,blob).
```

What is Prolog's response to the queries:

```
findall(X,q(blob,X),List).
findall(X,q(X,blug),List).
findall(X,q(X,Y),List).
bagof(X,q(X,Y),List).
setof(X,Y^q(X,Y),List).
```

Exercise 11.3.   Write a predicate sigma/2 that takes an integer $n > 0$ $\boxed{\mathcal{E}}$
and calculates the sum of all integers from 1 to n. For example:

```
?- sigma(3,X).
X = 6
yes
?- sigma(5,X).
X = 15
yes
```

Write the predicate so that results are stored in the database (there
should never be more than one entry in the database for each value)
and are reused whenever possible. For example, suppose we make the
following query:

```
?- sigma(2,X).
X = 3
yes
?- listing.
sigmares(2,3).
```

Then, if we go on to ask

```
?- sigma(3,X).
```

Prolog should not calculate everything new, but should get the result for
sigma(2,3) from the database and only add 3 to that. It should then
answer:

```
X = 6
yes
?- listing.
sigmares(2,3).
sigmares(3,6).
```

4 Practical Session

Try the following two programming exercises:

1. Sets can be thought of as lists that don't contain any repeated elements. For example, [a,4,6] is a set, but [a,4,6,a] is not (as it contains two occurrences of a). Write a Prolog program subset/2 that is satisfied when the first argument is a subset of the second argument (that is, when every element of the first argument is a member of the second argument). For example:

   ```
   ?- subset([a,b],[a,b,c])
   yes
   ```

   ```
   ?- subset([c,b],[a,b,c])
   yes
   ```

   ```
   ?- subset([],[a,b,c])
   yes
   ```

   Your program should be capable of generating all subsets of an input set by backtracking. For example, if you give it as input

   ```
   ?- subset(X,[a,b,c])
   ```

   it should successively generate all eight subsets of [a,b,c].

2. Using the subset predicate you have just written, and findall/3, write a predicate powerset/2 that takes a set as its first argument, and returns the powerset of this set as the second argument. (The powerset of a set is the set of all its subsets.) For example:

   ```
   ?- powerset([a,b,c],P)
   ```

   should return

   ```
   P = [[],[a],[b],[c],[a,b],[a,c],[b,c],[a,b,c]]
   ```

   It doesn't matter if the sets are returned in some other order. For example,

   ```
   P = [[a],[b],[c],[a,b,c],[],[a,b],[a,c],[b,c]]
   ```

   is fine too.

Chapter 12

Working With Files

This chapter is concerned with various aspect of
file handling and modularity. We will learn three
things:

1. How predicate definitions can be spread across
   different files.

2. How to write modular software systems.

3. How to write results to files and how to read
   input from files.

1   Splitting Programs over Files

By this stage you have written lots of programs that use the predicates append/3 and member/2. What you probably did each time you needed one of them was to go back to the definition and copy it over to the file where you wanted to use it. And maybe, after having done that a few times, you started thinking that it was quite annoying having to copy the same predicate definitions over and over again — how pleasant it would be if you could define them somewhere once and for all and then simply access them whenever you needed them. Well, that sounds like a pretty sensible thing to ask for and, of course, Prolog offers you ways of doing it.

Reading in programs

In fact, you already know a way of telling Prolog to read in predicate definitions that are stored in a file, namely the

    [FileName1]

consult

command. You have been using queries of this form all along to tell Prolog to consult files. But there are two more useful things you should know about it. First, you can consult many files at once by saying

    [FileName1,FileName2,...,FileNameN]

instead. Second, and more importantly, file consultation does *not* have to be performed interactively. If you put

    :- [FileName1,FileName2,...,FileNameN].

at the top of your program file (say main.pl) you are telling Prolog to first consult the listed files before going on to read in the rest of your program.

This feature gives us a simple way of re-using definitions. For example, suppose that you keep all the predicate definitions for basic list processing (such as append/3, member/2, reverse/2, and so on) in a file called listPredicates.pl. If you want to use them, simply put

    :- [listPredicates].

at the top of the file containing the program that needs them. Prolog will consult listPredicates when reading in that file, and all the predicate definitions in listPredicates become available.

There's one practical point you should be aware of. When Prolog loads files, it doesn't normally check whether the files really need to be consulted. If the predicate definitions provided by one of the files are already in the database because that file was consulted previously, Prolog will still consult it again, although it doesn't need to. This can be annoying if you are consulting very large files.

The built-in predicate ensure_loaded/1 behaves more intelligently in this respect. It works as follows. On encountering the following directive

```
:- ensure_loaded([listPredicates]).
```

Prolog checks whether the file listPredicates.pl has already been loaded and only loads it again if it has changed since the last loading.

Modules

Now imagine that you are writing a program that manages a movie database. You have designed a predicate printActors which displays all actors starring in a particular film, and a predicate printMovies which displays all movies directed by a particular filmmaker. Both definitions are stored in different files, namely printActors.pl and printMovies.pl, and both use an auxiliary predicate displayList/1. Here's the first file:

```
% This is the file: printActors.pl

printActors(Film):-
    setof(Actor,starring(Actor,Film),List),
    displayList(List).

displayList([]):- nl.
displayList([X|L]):-
    write(X), tab(1),
    displayList(L).
```

And here's the second:

```
% This is the file: printMovies.pl

printMovies(Director):-
    setof(Film,directed(Director,Film),List),
    displayList(List).

displayList([]):- nl.
displayList([X|L]):-
    write(X), nl,
    displayList(L).
```

Note that displayList/1 has different definitions in the two files:
the actors are printed in a row (using tab/1), and the films are printed
in a column (using nl/0). Will this lead to conflicts in Prolog? Let's
see. We'll load both programs by placing the statements

```
% This is the file: main.pl

:- [printActors].
:- [printMovies].
```

at the top of the main file. Consulting the main file will evoke a
message that looks something like the following:

```
?- [main].
{consulting main.pl...}
{consulting printActors.pl...}
{printActors.pl consulted, 10 msec 296 bytes}
{consulting printMovies.pl...}
The procedure displayList/1 is being redefined.
    Old file: printActors.pl
    New file: printMovies.pl
Do you really want to redefine it? (y, n, p, or ?)
```

What has happened? Well, as both files printActors.pl and
printMovies.pl define a predicate called displayList/1, Prolog needs
to choose one of the two definitions (it can't have two different
definitions for one predicate in its knowledge base).

What to do? Well, perhaps in some of these situations you really
do want to redefine a predicate. But here you don't — you want two
different definitions because you want movies and actors to be displayed
differently. One way of dealing with this is to give a different name to
one of the two predicates. But let's face it, this is clumsy. You want to
think of each file as a conceptually self-contained entity; you don't want
to waste time and energy thinking about how you named predicates in
some other file. And the most natural way of achieving the desired
conceptual independence is to use Prolog's module system.

| module system |

Modules essentially allow you to hide predicate definitions. You are
allowed to decide which predicates should be public (that is, callable

| public |

from parts of the program that are stored in other files) and which
predicates should be private (that is, callable only from within the

| private |

module itself). Thus you will not be able to call private predicates
from outside the module in which they are defined, but there will be

no conflicts if two modules internally define the same predicate. In our example, displayList/1 is a good candidate for becoming a private predicate; it plays a simple auxiliary role in both printActors/1 and printMovies/1, and the details of the role it plays for one predicate are not relevant to the other.

You can turn a file into a module by putting a module declaration at the top. Module declarations are of the form

> module
> declaration

```
:- module(ModuleName,
          List_of_Predicates_to_be_Exported).
```

Such declarations specify the name of the module and the list of public predicates, that is, the list of predicates that you want to export. These will be the only predicates that are accessible from outside the module.

> export

Let's modularise our movie database programs. We only need to include the following line at the top of the first file:

```
% This is the file: printActors.pl

:- module(printActors, [printActors/1]).

printActors(Film):-
    setof(Actor,starring(Actor,Film),List),
    displayList(List).

displayList([]):- nl.
displayList([X|L]):-
    write(X), tab(1),
    displayList(L).
```

Here we have introduced a module called printActors, with one public predicate printActors/1. The predicate displayList/1 is only known in the scope of the module printActors, so its definition won't affect any other modules.

Likewise we can turn the second file into a module:

```
% This is the file: printMovies.pl

:- module(printMovies, [printMovies/1]).

printMovies(Director):-
    setof(Film,directed(Director,Film),List),
    displayList(List).
```

```
displayList([]):- nl.
displayList([X|L]):-
    write(X), nl,
    displayList(L).
```

Again, the definition of the displayList/1 is only known in the scope of the module printMovies, so there won't be any clash when loading both modules at the same time.

Modules can be loaded with the built-in predicates use_module/1. This will import all predicates that were defined as public by the module. In other words, all public predicates will be accessible. To do this we need to change the main file as follows:

```
% This is the file: main.pl

:- use_module(printActors).
:- use_module(printMovies).
```

If you don't want to use all public predicates of a module, but only some of them, you can use the two-place version of use_module, which takes a list of predicates that you actually want to import as its second argument. So, by putting

```
% This is the file: main.pl

:- use_module(printActors,[printActors/1]).
:- use_module(printMovies,[printMovies/1]).
```

at the top of the main file, we have explicitly stated that we can use printActors/1 and printMovies/1, and nothing else (in this case, of course, the declaration is unnecessary as there are no other public predicates that we could use). Needless to say, you can only import predicates that are actually exported by the relevant module.

Libraries

Many of the most common predicates are provided predefined, in one way or another, by most Prolog implementations. If you have been using SWI Prolog, for example, you will probably have noticed that predicates like append/3 and member/2 come as part of the system. That's a speciality of SWI, however. Other Prolog implementations, like SICStus for example, don't have them built-in, but provide them as part of a library.

Libraries are modules defining common predicates, and can be loaded using the normal commands for importing modules. When specifying the name of the library that you want to use, you have to tell Prolog that this module is a library, so that Prolog knows where to look for it (namely, in the place where Prolog keeps its libraries, not in the directory where your other code is). For example, putting the directive

```
:- use_module(library(lists)).
```

at the top of your file tells Prolog to load a library called `lists`. In SICStus Prolog, this library contains a set of commonly used list processing predicates.

Libraries can be very useful and they can save you a lot of work. Moreover, the code in libraries has typically been written by excellent programmers, and is likely to be highly efficient and problem-free. However the way that libraries are organised and the inventory of predicates provided by libraries are by no means standardised across different Prolog implementations. This means that if you want your program to run with different Prolog implementations, it is probably easier and faster to define your own library modules (using the techniques that we saw in the last section) rather than to try to work around the incompatibilities between the library systems of different Prolog implementations.

2 Writing to Files

Many applications require that output be written to a file rather than to the screen. In this section we will explain how to do this in Prolog.

In order to write to a file we have to create one (or open an existing one) and associate a stream with it. You can think of streams as connections to files. In Prolog, streams are blessed with names in a rather user-unfriendly format, such as `'\$stream'(183368)`. Luckily, you never have to bother about the exact names of streams — although Prolog assigns these names internally, you can use Prolog's unification to match the name to a variable and make use of the variable rather than the name of the stream itself.

Say you want to print the string 'Hogwarts' to the file `hogwarts.txt`. This is done as follows:

```
...
open('hogwarts.txt',write,Stream),
write(Stream,'Hogwarts'), nl(Stream),
close(Stream),
...
```

What's happening here? Well, first the built-in predicate open/3 is used to create the file hogwarts.txt. The second argument of open/3 indicates that we want to open a new file (overwriting any existing file with the same name). The third argument of open/3 returns the name of the stream. Secondly, we write 'Hogwarts' on the stream and issue a newline command as well. After this we are ready, and close the stream, using the built-in close/1.

open

write

close

And that's more or less all there is to it. As promised, we were not interested in the name of the stream — we used the variable Stream to pass it around. Also note that the write/2 predicate we used here is basically a more general form of the write/1 predicates we used in Chapter 9 for writing to the screen.

append

What if you don't want to overwrite an existing file but append to an existing one? This is done by choosing a different mode when opening the file: instead of write, use append as value for the second argument of open/3. If a file of the given name doesn't exist, it will be created.

3 Reading from Files

In this section we show how to read from files. Reading information from files is straightforward in Prolog — or at least, it is if this information is given in the form of Prolog terms followed by full stops. Consider the file houses.txt:

```
gryffindor.
hufflepuff.
ravenclaw.
slytherin.
```

Here is a Prolog program that opens this file, reads the information from it, and displays it on the screen:

```
main:-
    open('houses.txt',read,Str),
    read(Str,House1),
    read(Str,House2),
    read(Str,House3),
    read(Str,House4),
    close(Str),
    write([House1,House2,House3,House4]), nl.
```

reading
mode

This opens a file in reading mode, then reads four Prolog terms using the built-in predicate read/2, closes the stream, and prints the information as a list.

All very straightforward. Nonetheless, the read/2 predicate needs to be handled with care. First of all, it only is able to handle Prolog terms (we'll say more about this problem shortly). And secondly, it will cause a run-time error if we use it to read from a stream when there is nothing to read. Is there an elegant way to overcome this second problem?

There is. The built-in predicate at_end_of_stream/1 checks whether the end of a stream has been reached, and can be used as a safety-net. For a stream X, at_end_of_stream(X) will evaluate to true when the end of the stream X is reached (in other words, when all terms in the corresponding file have been read).

| end of a |
| stream |

The following code is a modified version of our earlier reading-in program, which shows how at_end_of_stream/1 can be incorporated:

```
main:-
    open('houses.txt',read,Str),
    read_houses(Str,Houses),
    close(Str),
    write(Houses), nl.

read_houses(Stream,[]):-
    at_end_of_stream(Stream).

read_houses(Stream,[X|L]):-
    \+ at_end_of_stream(Stream),
    read(Stream,X),
    read_houses(Stream,L).
```

Now for the nastier problem. Recall that read/2 only reads in Prolog terms. If you want to read in arbitrary input, things become rather unpleasant, as Prolog forces you to read information on the level of characters. The predicate that you need in this case is get_code/2 which reads the next available character from a stream. Characters are represented in Prolog by their integer codes. For example, get_code/2 will return 97 if the next character on the stream is an a.

Usually we are not interested in these integer codes, but in the characters — or rather, in the atoms that are made up of lists of these characters. How do we get our hands on these (lists of) characters? One way is to use the built-in predicate atom_codes/2 that we introduced in Chapter 9 to convert a list of integers into the corresponding atom. We'll use this technique in the following example, a predicate that reads in a word from a stream.

```
readWord(InStream,W):-
  get_code(InStream,Char),
  checkCharAndReadRest(Char,Chars,InStream),
  atom_codes(W,Chars).


checkCharAndReadRest(10,[],_):- !.

checkCharAndReadRest(32,[],_):- !.

checkCharAndReadRest(-1,[],_):- !.

checkCharAndReadRest(end_of_file,[],_):- !.

checkCharAndReadRest(Char,[Char|Chars],InStream):-
  get_code(InStream,NextChar),
  checkCharAndReadRest(NextChar,Chars,InStream).
```

How does this work? It reads in a character and then checks whether this character is a blank (integer code 32), a new line (10) or the end of the stream (−1). In any of these cases a complete word has been read, otherwise the next character is read.

4 Exercises

Exercise 12.1.   Write code that creates hogwart.houses, a file that that looks like this:

```
      gryffindor
hufflepuff      ravenclaw
      slytherin
```

You can use the built-in predicates open/3, close/1, tab/2, nl/1, and write/2.

Exercise 12.2.   Write a Prolog program that reads in a plain text file word by word, and asserts all read words and their frequency into the Prolog database. You may use the predicate readWord/2 to read in words. Use a dynamic predicate word/2 to store the words, where the first argument is a word, and the second argument is the frequency of that word.

5 Practical Session

In this practical session, we want to combine what we have learned about file handling with some topics we met in earlier chapters. The goal is to write a program for running a DCG grammar on a testsuite, so that the performance of the grammar can be checked.

What is a testsuite? It is a file that contains lots of possible inputs (and expected outputs) for some program. In this case, a testsuite will be a file that has lists representing grammatical and ungrammatical sentences, such as [the,woman,shoots,the,cow,under,the,shower] or [him,shoots,woman]. The test program should take this file, run the grammar on each of the sentences, and store the results in another file. We can then look at the output file to check whether the grammar answered everywhere the way it should have. When developing grammars, testsuites like this are extremely useful for making sure that any modifications we make to the grammar don't have unwanted effects.

Step 1

Take the DCG that you built in the practical session of Chapter 8 and turn it into a module, exporting the predicate s/3, that is, the predicate that lets you parse sentences and returns the parse tree as its first argument.

Step 2

In the practical session of Chapter 9, you had to write a program for pretty printing parse trees onto the screen. Turn that into a module as well.

Step 3

Now modify the program so that it prints the tree not to the screen but to a given stream. That means that the predicate pptree should now be a two-place predicate taking the Prolog representation of a parse tree and a stream as arguments.

Step 4

Import both modules into a file and define a two-place predicate test which takes a list representing a sentence (such as [a,woman,shoots]), parses it, and writes the result to the file specified by the second argument of test. Check that everything is working as it should.

Step 5

Finally, modify test/2, so that it takes a filename instead of a sentence as its first argument, reads in the sentences given in the file one by one,

parses them, and writes the sentence as well as the parsing result into
the output file. For example, if your input file looked like this:

    [the,cow,under,the,table,shoots].

    [a,dead,woman,likes,he].

the output file should look something like this:

    [the, cow, under, the, table, shoots]

```
      s(
        np(
           det(the)
           nbar(
              n(cow))
           pp(
              prep(under)
              np(
                 det(the)
                 nbar(
                    n(table)))))
        vp(
           v(shoots)))
```

    [a, dead, woman, likes, he]

    no

Step 6

Now (if you are in for some real Prolog hacking) try to write a module
that reads in sentences terminated by a full stop or a line break from a
file, so that you can give your testsuite as

    the cow under the table shoots .

    a dead woman likes he .

instead of

    [the,cow,under,the,table,shoots].

    [a,dead,woman,likes,he].

Step 7

Make the testsuite environment more sophisticated, by adding information to the input file about the expected output (in this case, whether the sentences has a parse or not). Then modify the program so that it checks whether the expected output matches the obtained output.

Answers to the Exercises

Yes, yes, you're right. We *did* put in the answers to all the exercises. Reluctantly and against our better judgement. Foolishly bowing to immense pressure. And now you've gone and found them...

But just because we've done something dumb, it doesn't mean you have to too. Once you have seen the answer to an exercise, you'll lose forever the chance of working it out yourself. But you've still got time to put things right. So don't turn this page! Go back and try again!

Didn't you hear what we just said?
This really is your very last chance!

Answer 1.1

1. vINCENT is an atom: it starts with a lower-case letter.

2. Footmassage is a variable: it starts with an upper-case letter.

3. variable23 is an atom: it starts with a lower-case letter.

4. Variable2000 is a variable: it starts with an uppercase letter.

5. big_kahuna_burger is an atom: it starts with a lower-case letter.

6. 'big kahuna burger' is an atom: it is between two single quotes.

7. big kahuna burger is neither: variables can never contain spaces, and atoms cannot either — unless the atom starts and ends with a single quote.

8. 'Jules' is an atom: it is enclosed between single quotes.

9. _Jules is a variable: it starts with an underscore.

10. '_Jules' is an atom: it is enclosed between single quotes.

Answer 1.2

1. loves(Vincent,mia) is a complex term. Its functor is loves and its arity is 2.

2. 'loves(Vincent,mia)' is an atom: it is enclosed between single quotes.

3. Butch(boxer) is not a term. It starts with an upper-case letter and therefore cannot be an atom or a complex term. It cannot be a variable either because variables are not supposed to contain parentheses.

4. boxer(Butch) is a complex term. Its functor is boxer and its arity is 1.

5. and(big(burger),kahuna(burger)) is a complex term. Its functor is and and its arity is 2. The arguments are again complex terms.

6. and(big(X),kahuna(X)) is a complex term. Its functor is and and its arity 2.

7. _and(big(X),kahuna(X)) is not a term. It starts with an
   underscore and can therefore not be an atom or a complex term.
   It cannot be a variable either because variables are not supposed
   to contain parentheses or commas.

8. (Butch kills Vincent) is not a term. It contains parentheses
   and empty spaces and therefore can neither be an atom nor a
   variable. It doesn't have the right format for a complex term
   either; in particular, it has no functor.

9. kills(Butch Vincent) is not a term. However, adding a comma
   between Butch and Vincent would make it into a complex term.

10. kills(Butch,Vincent is not a term. However, adding a closing
    parenthesis at the end would make it into a complex term.

Answer 1.3

There are three facts and four rules in this knowledge base. This means
that there are seven clauses. The heads of the rules are person(X),
loves(X,Y), and father(Y,Z) (everything on the left-hand side of
the rules), the goals are man(X), woman(X), knows(Y,X), man(Y),
son(Z,Y), and daughter(Z,Y) (everything on the right hand side of
the rules). This knowledge base defines five predicates, namely woman/1,
man/1, person/1, loves/2, and father/2.

Answer 1.4

Here is an example of what your answers could look like. They, of
course, don't have to look *exactly* like that. For example, the first fact
could also be killer('Butch') or killer(b) or even $k(50)$, if you
decide to represent Butch by the number 50 and the property of being
a killer by the predicate k/1.

1.   killer(butch).

2.   married(mia, marsellus).

3.   dead(zed).

4.   kill(marsellus,X):- give(X,mia,Y), footmassage(Y).

5.   love(mia,X):- good_dancer(X).

6.   eat(jules,X):- nutritious(X).
      eat(jules,X):- tasty(X).

Answer 1.5

1.     ```
       ?- wizard(ron).
       yes
       ```

2.     ```
       ?- witch(ron).
       no
       ```

   or

       ```
       ERROR: Undefined procedure: witch/1
       ```

3.     ```
       ?- wizard(hermione).
       no
       ```

4.     ```
       ?- witch(hermione).
       no
       ```

   or

       ```
       ERROR: Undefined procedure: witch/1
       ```

5.     ```
       ?- wizard(harry).
       yes
       ```

6.     ```
       ?- wizard(Y).
       Y = ron ;
       Y = harry ;
       no
       ```

7.     ```
       ?- witch(Y).
       no
       ```

   or

       ```
       ERROR: Undefined procedure: witch/1
       ```

Answer 2.1

1. bread = bread unifies.

2. 'Bread' = bread doesn't unify.

3. 'bread' = bread unifies.

4. Bread = bread unifies; the variable Bread gets instantiated with the atom bread.
       ```

5. bread = sausage doesn't unify.

6. food(bread) = bread doesn't unify.

7. food(bread) = X unifies; X gets instantiated with food(bread).

8. food(X) = food(bread) unifies; X gets instantiated with bread.

9. food(bread,X) = food(Y,sausage) unifies; X gets instantiated with sausage and Y gets instantiated with bread.

10. food(bread,X,beer) = food(Y,sausage,X) doesn't unify; X cannot be instantiated with sausage as well as beer.

11. food(bread,X,beer) = food(Y,kahuna_burger) doesn't unify; the functors are of different arity.

12. food(X) = X is trickier. According to the basic definition of unification given in the text, these two terms do not unify, as no matter what (finite) term we instantiate X to, the two sides won't be identical. However (as we mentioned in the text) modern Prolog interpreters will detect that there is a problem here and will instantiate X with the 'infinite term' food(food(food(...))), and report that unification succeeds. In short, there is no 'correct' answer to this question; it's essentially a matter of convention. The important point is to understand why such unifications need to be handled with care.

13. meal(food(bread),drink(beer)) = meal(X,Y) unifies; X gets instantiated with food(bread) and Y with drink(beer).

14. meal(food(bread),X) = meal(X,drink(beer)) doesn't unify; X cannot get instantiated twice with different things.

Answer 2.2

1.   ?- magic(house_elf). no

2.   ?- wizard(harry).
      no

   or

      ERROR: undefined procedure wizard/1

3.   ?- magic(wizard).
      no

4.   ?- magic('McGonagall').
      yes

5.   ?- magic(Hermione).
      Hermione = dobby ;
      Hermione = hermione ;
      Hermione = 'McGonagall' ;
      Hermione = rita_skeeter ;
      no

The search tree for the last query is:

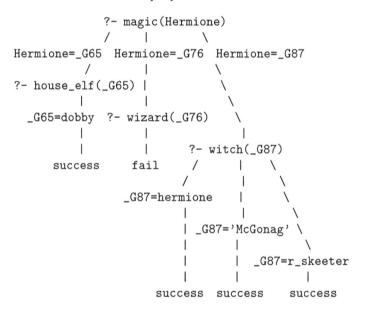

Answer 2.3

    ?- sentence(W1,W2,W3,W4,W5).
    W1 = a,
    W2 = criminal,
    W3 = eats,
    W4 = a,
    W5 = criminal ;

    W1 = a,
    W2 = criminal,
    W3 = eats,

```
W4 = a,
W5 = 'big kahuna burger' ;

W1 = a,
W2 = criminal,
W3 = eats,
W4 = every,
W5 = criminal ;

W1 = a,
W2 = criminal,
W3 = eats,
W4 = every,
W5 = 'big kahuna burger' ;

W1 = a,
W2 = criminal,
W3 = likes,
W4 = a,
W5 = 'criminal' ;

W1 = a,
W2 = criminal,
W3 = likes,
W4 = a,
W5 = 'big kahuna burger' ;

W1 = a,
W2 = criminal,
W3 = likes,
W4 = every,
W5 = criminal ;

W1 = a,
W2 = criminal,
W3 = likes,
W4 = every,
W5 = 'big kahuna burger' ;

W1 = a,
W2 = 'big kahuna burger',
```

```
W3 = eats,
W4 = a,
W5 = criminal ;


        .
        .
        .


W1 = every,
W2 = 'big kahuna burger',
W3 = likes,
W4 = every,
W5 = 'big kahuna burger' ;
no
```

Answer 2.4

```
crossword(V1,V2,V3,H1,H2,H3):-
   word(V1,_,A,_,B,_,C,_),
   word(V2,_,D,_,E,_,F,_),
   word(V3,_,G,_,H,_,I,_),
   word(H1,_,A,_,D,_,G,_),
   word(H2,_,B,_,E,_,H,_),
   word(H3,_,C,_,F,_,I,_).
```

Answer 3.1

No, it's not a good idea to reformulate descend/2 in that way: it
will get in an infinite loop for certain queries. For example, if one
queries ?- descend(rose,X), the first clause will fail, but the second
clause applies. But the second clause tries to find a solution for ?-
descend(rose,Z), and so on.

Answer 3.2

```
directlyIn(irina,natasha).
directlyIn(natasha,olga).
directlyIn(olga,katarina).

in(X,Y):- directlyIn(X,Y).
in(X,Y):- directlyIn(X,Z), in(Z,Y).
```

Answer 3.3

```
travelFromTo(X,Y):-
   directTrain(X,Y).
```

```
travelFromTo(X,Y):-
   directTrain(X,Z),
   travelFromTo(Z,Y).
```

Answer 3.4

```
greater_than(succ(X),0).
greater_than(succ(X),succ(Y)):- greater_than(X,Y).
```

Answer 3.5

```
swap(leaf(X),leaf(X)).
swap(tree(B1,B2),tree(B2Swapped,B1Swapped)):-
   swap(B1,B1Swapped),
   swap(B2,B2Swapped).
```

Answer 4.1

1.   `?- [a,b,c,d] = [a,[b,c,d]].`
    No

    (The first list has four elements; the second only two.)

2.   `?- [a,b,c,d] = [a|[b,c,d]].`
    Yes

3.   `?- [a,b,c,d] = [a,b,[c,d]].`
    No

4.   `?- [a,b,c,d] = [a,b|[c,d]].`
    Yes

5.   `?- [a,b,c,d] = [a,b,c,[d]].`
    No

6.   `?- [a,b,c,d] = [a,b,c|[d]].`
    Yes

7.   `?- [a,b,c,d] = [a,b,c,d,[]].`
    No

8.   `?- [a,b,c,d] = [a,b,c,d|[]].`
    Yes

9.   `?- [] = _.`
    Yes
```
```

10.   ?- [] = [_].
           No

   (The first list is empty; the second list has one element.)

11.   ?- [] = [_|[]].
           No

   (The first list is empty; the second list has one element.)

Answer 4.2

1. [1|[2,3,4]] is correct. The list has four elements.

2. [1,2,3|[]] is correct. The list has three elements.

3. [1|2,3,4] is not correct. The tail, that is, what's right of |, has to be a list (as in the first example) but it's not.

4. [1|[2|[3|[4]]]] is correct. The list has four elements.

5. [1,2,3,4|[]] is correct. The list has four elements.

6. [[]|[]] is correct. The list has one element, namely the empty list.

7. [[1,2]|4] is not correct. The tail is not a list.

8. [[1,2],[3,4]|[5,6,7]] is correct. The list has five elements.

Answer 4.3

    second(X,[_,X|_]).

Answer 4.4

    swap12([H1,H2|T],[H2,H1|T]).

Answer 4.5

The base clause: the input list is empty. There is nothing to translate, so the output list is empty as well.

    listtran([],[]).

The recursive clause: we translate the head G of the input list using the predicate tran/2. The result is E and becomes the head of the output list. Then we recursively translate the rest of the input. The result becomes the rest of the output.

    listtran([G|GT],[E|ET]):-
        tran(G,E),
        listtran(GT,ET).

Answer 4.6

The base clause: the input list is empty. So there is nothing to write to the output list. So that is empty as well.

```
twice([],[]).
```

The recursive clause: the first two elements of the output list are both identical to the head of the input list. The recursive call simply produces the tail of the output list from the tail of the input list.

```
twice([H|TIn],[H,H|TOut]):-
    twice(TIn, TOut).
```

Answer 4.7

```
?- member(a,[c,b,a,y]).
        |
?- member(a,[b,a,y])
        |
 ?- member(a,[a,y])
        |
            success

?- member(x,[a,b,c]).
        |
?- member(x,[b,c]).
        |
 ?- member(x,[c]).
        |
  ?- member(x,[]).
        |
            fail

?- member(X,[a,b,c]).
     /              \
  X=a                X=_G65
   |                  |
  success    ?-member(_G65,[b,c]).
           /                  \
     _G65=b      ?- member(_G65,[c])
        |                      |
     success                _G65=c
                               |
                            success
```

Answer 5.1

1. Prolog answers: X = 3*4. Variable X is instantiated with the complex term 3*4.

2. Prolog answers: X = 12.

3. Prolog answers: ERROR: Arguments are not sufficiently instantiated.

4. Prolog answers: X = Y.

5. Prolog answers: yes.

6. Prolog answers: yes.

7. Prolog answers: ERROR: Arguments are not sufficiently instantiated.

8. Prolog answers: X = 3.

9. Prolog answers: no. Prolog evaluates the arithmetic expression to the right of is/2. Then it tries to unify the result with the term to the left of is/2. This fails as the number 3 does not unify the complex term 1+2.

10. Prolog answers: X = 3.

11. Prolog answers: yes. 3+2 and +(3,2) are two ways of writing the same term.

12. Prolog answers: yes.

13. Prolog answers: yes.

14. Prolog answers: yes.

15. Prolog answers: no.

16. Prolog answers: yes.

Answer 5.2

```
increment(X,Y):-
    Y is X + 1.

sum(X,Y,Z):-
    Z is X + Y.
```

Answer 5.3

```
addone([],[]).

addone([H|T],[H1|T1]):-
    H1 is H + 1,
    addone(T,T1).
```

Answer 6.1

```
doubled(L):-
    append(L1,L1,L).
```

Answer 6.2

A solution using reverse/2:

```
palindrome(L):-
    reverse(L,L).
```

A solution using no built-in predicates:

```
palindrome(L):-
    check_palindrome(L,[]).

check_palindrome(L,L).

check_palindrome([_|L],L).

check_palindrome([H|T],LPal):-
    check_palindrome(T,[H|LPal]).
```

Answer 6.3

```
toptail([H|TInList],OutList):-
    append(OutList,[_],TInList).
```

Answer 6.4

A solution using reverse/2:

```
last(L,X):-
    reverse(L,[X|_]).
```

An alternative solution:

```
last([X],X).

last([_|L],X):-
    last(L,X).
```

Answer 6.5

A solution using append/3:

```
swapfl([H1|T1],[H2|T2]):-
    append(Middle,[H2],T1),
    append(Middle,[H1],T2).
```

An alternative solution:

```
swapfl([First,Last],[Last,First]).

swapfl([First,Next|L1],[Last,Next|L2]):-
    swapfl([First|L1],[Last|L2]).
```

Answer 6.6

In this solution the street is represented as list of three houses. A house is represented as a 3-place (colour, nationality, pet) complex term. With the help of member/2 and sublist/2 we check the constraints of the puzzle.

```
zebra(N) :-
 Street = [House1,House2,House3],
 member(house(red,_,_),Street),
 member(house(blue,_,_),Street),
 member(house(green,_,_),Street),
 member(house(red,english,_),Street),
 member(house(_,spanish,jaguar),Street),
 sublist([house(_,_,snail),house(_,japanese,_)],Street),
 sublist([house(blue,_,_),house(_,_,snail)],Street),
 member(house(_,N,zebra),Street).
```

Answer 7.1

The internal representation of the DCG rules that Prolog will work with:

```
s(A,B) :- foo(A,C), bar(C,D), wiggle(D,B).
foo([choo|A],A).
foo(A,B) :- foo(A,C), foo(C,B).
bar(A,B) :- mar(A,C), zar(C,B).
mar(A,B) :- me(A,C), my(C,B).
me([i|A],A).
my([am|A],A).
zar(A,B) :- blar(A,C), car(C,B),
blar([a|A],A).
```

```
car([train|A],A).
wiggle([toot|A],A).
wiggle(A,B) :- wiggle(A,C), wriggle(C,B).
```

The first three sentences that Prolog will generate:

1. choo i am a train toot

2. choo i am a train toot toot

3. choo i am a train toot toot toot

Answer 7.2

```
s --> [a,b].
s --> a, s, b.
a --> [a].
b --> [b].
```

Answer 7.3

```
s --> [].
s --> a, s, b.
a --> [a].
b --> [b,b].
```

Answer 8.1

```
s --> np(Num),vp(Num).

np(Num) --> det,n(Num).

vp(Num) --> v(Num),np(_).
vp(Num) --> v(Num).

det --> [the].
det --> [a].

n(sg) --> [woman].
n(pl) --> [women].
n(sg) --> [man].
n(pl) --> [men].
n(sg) --> [apple].
n(pl) --> [apples].
n(sg) --> [pear].
n(pl) --> [pears].
```

```
v(sg) --> [eats].
v(pl) --> [eat].
```

Answer 8.2

```
kanga(A,B,C,D,E):-
   roo(A,B,D,F),
   jumps(C,C,F,G),
   marsupial(A,B,C),
   E=G.
```

Answer 9.1

1. The query ?- 12 is 2*6. succeeds.

2. The query ?- 14 =\= 2*6. succeeds.

3. The query ?- 14 = 2*7. fails.

4. The query ?- 14 == 2*7. fails.

5. The query ?- 14 \== 2*7. succeeds.

6. The query ?- 14 =:= 2*7. succeeds.

7. The query ?- [1,2,3|[d,e]] == [1,2,3,d,e]. succeeds.

8. The query ?- 2+3 == 3+2. fails.

9. The query ?- 2+3 =:= 3+2. succeeds.

10. The query ?- 7-2 =\= 9-2. succeeds.

11. The query ?- p == 'p'. succeeds.

12. The query ?- p =\= 'p'. yields an error.

13. The query ?- vincent == VAR. fails.

14. The query ?- vincent=VAR, VAR==vincent. succeeds.

Answer 9.2

1. The query ?- .(a,.(b,.(c,[]))) = [a,b,c]. succeeds.

2. The query ?- .(a,.(b,.(c,[]))) = [a,b|[c]]. succeeds.

3. The query ?- .(.(a,[]),.(.(b,[]),.(.(c,[]),[])))=X. succeeds and and X = [[a],[b],[c]].

4. The query ?- .(a,.(b,.(.(c,[]),[]))) = [a,b|[c]]. fails.

Answer 9.3

```
termtype(Term,variable):-
   var(Term).

termtype(Term,atom):-
   atom(Term).

termtype(Term,number):-
   number(Term).

termtype(Term,constant):-
   atomic(Term).

termtype(Term,simple_term):-
   atomic(Term).

termtype(Term,simple_term):-
   var(Term).

termtype(Term,complex_term):-
   nonvar(Term),
   functor(Term,_,Arity),
   Arity > 0.

termtype(Term,term):-
   termtype(Term,simple_term).

termtype(Term,term):-
   termtype(Term,complex_term).
```

Answer 9.4

First, a solution that doesn't use univ:

```
groundterm(Term):-
   atomic(Term).

groundterm(Term):-
   nonvar(Term),
   functor(Term,_,Arity),
   groundterms(Term,Arity).

groundterms(_,0).
```

```
groundterms(ComplexTerm,Arg):-
    Arg > 0,
    arg(Arg,ComplexTerm,Term),
    groundterm(Term),
    NextArg is Arg - 1,
    groundterms(ComplexTerm,NextArg).
```

And here is a solution that does use univ:

```
groundterm(Term) :-
        atomic(Term).
groundterm(Term) :-
        nonvar(Term),
        Term =.. [_|Args],
        groundterms(Args).

groundterms([]).
groundterms([H|T]) :-
        groundterm(H),
        groundterms(T).
```

Answer 9.5

Given these operator definitions,

1. `X is_a witch` corresponds to the Prolog term `is_a(X,witch)`;

2. `harry and ron and hermione are friends` corresponds to the Prolog term `are(and(harry,and(ron,hermione)),friends)`;

3. `harry is_a wizard and likes quidditch` is not a Prolog term;

4. `dumbledore is_a famous wizard` corresponds to the Prolog term `isa_a(dumbledore,famous(wizard))`.

Answer 10.1

```
?- p(X).
X = 1 ;
X = 2 ;
No

?- p(X), p(Y).
X = 1
Y = 1 ;
```

```
X = 1
Y = 2 ;
X = 2
Y = 1 ;
X = 2
Y = 2 ;
No

?- p(X), !, p(Y).
X = 1
Y = 1 ;
X = 1
Y = 2 ;
No
```

Answer 10.2

The original program tells whether a number is positive, zero, or negative. It does that using three clauses. But if one of the three clauses succeeds in solving a goal, the others do not apply. Hence we can add green cuts:

```
class(Number,positive):- Number > 0, !.
class(0,zero):- !.
class(Number,negative):- Number < 0, !.
```

Answer 10.3

A version of split/3 without using the cut:

```
split([],[],[]).

split([Number|L],[X|Pos],Neg):-
   Number >= 0,
   split(L,Pos,Neg).

split([Number|L],Pos,[X|Neg]):-
   Number < 0,
   split(L,Pos,Neg).
```

A version of split/3 using the cut:

```
split([],[],[]):- !.
```

```
split([Number|L],[X|Pos],Neg):-
   Number > 0, !,
   split(L,Pos,Neg).

split([Number|L],[X|Pos],Neg):-
   Number = 0, !,
   split(L,Pos,Neg).

split([Number|L],Pos,[X|Neg]):-
   Number < 0, !,
   split(L,Pos,Neg).
```

Answer 10.4

```
directTrain(saarbruecken,dudweiler).
directTrain(forbach,saarbruecken).
directTrain(freyming,forbach).
directTrain(stAvold,freyming).
directTrain(fahlquemont,stAvold).
directTrain(metz,fahlquemont).
directTrain(nancy,metz).

trainConnection(A,B):- directTrain(A,B).
trainConnection(A,B):- directTrain(B,A).

route(A,B,Route):-
   route(B,A,[B],Route).

route(A,B,Route,[B|Route]):-
   trainConnection(A,B),
   \+ member(B,Route).

route(A,C,SoFar,Route):-
   trainConnection(A,B),
   \+ member(B,SoFar),
   route(B,C,[B|SoFar],Route).
```

Answer 11.1

After the first query the database contains:

```
q(foo,blug).
q(a,b).
q(1,2).
```

After the second command the database contains:

```
q(foo,blug).
q(a,b).
p(X):- h(X).
```

After the third command the database contains:

```
p(X):- h(X).
```

Answer 11.2

1.  ```
    List = [blug,blag,blig] ;
    No
    ```

2.  ```
    List = [blob,dang] ;
    No
    ```

3.  ```
    List = [blob,blob,blob,blaf,dang,dang,flab] ;
    No
    ```

4.  ```
    List = [blob] ;
    Y = blag
    List = [blob,blaf] ;
    Y = dong
    List = [dang] ;
    Y = blug
    List = [blob,dang] ;
    Y = blob
    List = [flab] ;
    No
    ```

5.  ```
    List = [blaf,blob,dang,flab] ;
    No
    ```

Answer 11.3

```
:- dynamic sigmares/2.

sigmares(0,0).

sigma(Number,Sum):-
    sigmares(Number,Sum).

sigma(Number,Total):-
```
```

```
    Number > 0,
    \+ sigmares(Number,Total),
    NewNumber is Number - 1,
    sigma(NewNumber,SubTotal),
    Total is SubTotal + Number,
    assert(sigmares(Number,Total)).
```

Answer 12.1

```
piece_of_code:-
    open('hogwart.houses',write,Stream),
    tab(Stream,6),
    write(Stream,gryffindor),
    nl(Stream),
    write(Stream,hufflepuf),
    tab(Stream,6),
    write(Stream,ravenclaw),
    nl(Stream),
    tab(Stream,6),
    write(Stream,slytherin),
    nl(Stream),
    close(Stream).
```

Answer 12.2

```
:- dynamic word/2.

readWord(Stream,W,Status):-
    get_code(Stream,Char),
    checkCharAndReadRest(Char,Chars,Stream,Status),
    atom_codes(W,Chars).

checkCharAndReadRest(10,[],_,ok):- !.
checkCharAndReadRest(32,[],_,ok):- !.
checkCharAndReadRest(-1,[],_,eof):- !.
checkCharAndReadRest(end_of_file,[],_,eof):- !.
checkCharAndReadRest(Char,[Char|Chars],Stream,Status):-
    get_code(Stream,NextChar),
    checkCharAndReadRest(NextChar,Chars,Stream,Status).

read_text(File):-
    open(File,read,Stream),
    read_words(Stream,ok),
    close(Stream).
```

```
read_words(_,eof).

read_words(Stream,PrevStatus):-
   \+ PrevStatus = eof,
   readWord(Stream,Word,Status),
   addWord(Word),
   read_words(Stream,Status).

addWord(Word):-
   word(Word,Freq), !,
   retract( word(Word,Freq) ),
   NewFreq is Freq + 1,
   assert( word(Word,NewFreq) ).

addWord(Word):-
   assert( word(Word,1) ).
```

Further Reading

While we think *Learn Prolog Now!* is a good first book on Prolog, it certainly shouldn't be the last one you look at. To help you take the next step, we have listed, with comments, some of our favourite Prolog textbooks, and Prolog-based books on Artificial Intelligence (AI) and Natural Language Processing (NLP).

Prolog textbooks

- Bratko (1990): *Prolog Programming for Artificial Intelligence*. Addison-Wesley. We strongly recommend this book. If you liked *Learn Prolog Now!* we think you'll find this a natural followup. Its strong point is the wide variety of programming styles and applications it considers. This is a big book, and it will take you quite a while to work through it. But if you do so, you'll soon be writing very substantial Prolog programs indeed, and you'll learn a lot about AI along the way.

- Clocksin (2003): *Clause and Effect: Prolog Programming for the Working Programmer*. Springer. Strongly recommended. If you want a concise practically oriented follow up to *Learn Prolog Now!* that will really hone your Prolog skills, you can't do better than this. It explains some interesting theory, but its real strength is that it is based around a collection of worksheets. Solve the problems they contain, and you'll soon be flying.

- Clocksin and Mellish (1987): *Programming in Prolog*. Springer. This was one of the earliest, if not the earliest, textbook on Prolog programming. It won't take you far beyond *Learn Prolog Now!*, but it is clearly written, and its discussions of DCGs, and of the link between logic and Prolog, are accessible and worth looking at.

- O'Keefe (1990): *Craft of Prolog*. MIT Press. This is the book you should read when you're convinced that you know all about Prolog and have nothing left to learn. Unless you truly are a Prolog guru, you will swiftly learn that there are far deeper levels of Prolog expertise than you suspected, and that you still have a great deal to master. Superb.

- Sterling (1994): *The Art of Prolog.* MIT Press. In *Learn Prolog Now!* we don't say much about the abstract idea of logic programming. If the little we have said has wakened your interest, this is the book to go for next. Clearly written, it will give you a good grounding in the basic theory of logic programming, and link it to the practical world of Prolog.

Applying Prolog in AI and NLP

- Blackburn and Bos (2005): *Representation and Inference for Natural Language. A First Course in Computational Semantics.* CSLI Lecture Notes. Introduces natural language semantics from a computational perspective using Prolog as the implementation language. *Learn Prolog Now!* was originally intended to be an appendix to this book.

- Covington (1994): *Natural Language Processing for Prolog Programmers.* Prentice-Hall. Solid, well-written book on NLP that uses Prolog as the implementation language. If you haven't done any NLP before, and want to put your Prolog to work, this is a good place to start.

- Pereira and Shieber (1987): *Prolog and Natural Language Analysis.* CSLI Lecture Notes. A classic. Several generations of PhD students have cut their teeth on this one. Required reading.

- Reiter (2001): *Knowledge in Action: Logical Foundations for Specifying and Implementing Dynamical Systems.* MIT Press. This book examines, extends, and implements the Situation Calculus, a well known AI formalism for representing and reasoning about changing information. It's an important book, and may not be completely accessible if you don't have some theoretical background. But as an example of how Prolog can be put to work, it takes some beating.

- Shoham (1994): *Artificial Intelligence Techniques in Prolog.* Morgan Kaufman. Discusses and implements a wide range of AI problem-solving techniques and concepts, including depth-first search, breadth-first search, best-first search, alpha-beta minimax, forward chaining, production systems, reasoning with uncertainty, and STRIPS.

Prolog Environments

Several Prolog environments are available, and probably the best idea is simply to google what's available. But we list here four of the more widely used systems.

- **SWI-Prolog**
  A Free Software Prolog environment, licensed under the Lesser GNU public license. This popular interpreter was developed by Jan Wielemaker.
  http://www.swi-prolog.org/

- **SICStus Prolog**
  Industrial strength Prolog environment from the Swedish Institute of Computer Science.
  http://www.sics.se/sicstus/

- **YAP Prolog**
  A Prolog compiler developed at the Universidade do Porto and Universidade Federa do Rio de Janeiro. Free for use in academic environments.
  http://www.ncc.up.pt/~vsc/Yap/

- **Ciao Prolog**
  Another Prolog environment available under the GNU public license, developed at the Universidad Politécnica de Madrid.
  http://clip.dia.fi.upm.es/Software/Ciao/

Predicate Index

Subject Index